THE
unofficial GUIDE®
TO Walt Disney World®

2018

D0976285

COME CHECK US OUT!

Supplement your valuable guidebook with tips, news, and deals by visiting our websites:

theunofficialguides.com
touringplans.com

Sign up for the Unofficial Guide newsletter for even more travel tips and special offers.

Join the conversation on social media:

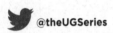 @theUGSeries    theUnofficialGuides

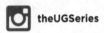 theUGSeries   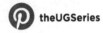 theUGSeries

#theUGseries

Other Unofficial Guides

Beyond Disney: The Unofficial Guide to SeaWorld, Universal Orlando, & the Best of Central Florida

The Disneyland Story: The Unofficial Guide to the Evolution of Walt Disney's Dream

Universal vs. Disney: The Unofficial Guide to American Theme Parks' Greatest Rivalry

The Unofficial Guide Color Companion to Walt Disney World

The Unofficial Guide to Disney Cruise Line

The Unofficial Guide to Disneyland

The Unofficial Guide to Las Vegas

The Unofficial Guide to Mall of America

The Unofficial Guide to Universal Orlando

The Unofficial Guide to Washington, DC

PART FIFTEEN

BEHIND-THE-SCENES *and* VIP TOURS *at* WALT DISNEY WORLD

IF YOU'RE INTERESTED IN THE MOUSE'S INNARDS — um, make that inner workings—a number of tours offer a glimpse of what goes on behind the scenes. Reservations must be guaranteed with a credit card, and you must cancel at least 48 hours in advance for a full refund. Many tours require that you also buy park admission; we note where it isn't mandatory. Prices include sales tax.

unofficial **TIP**
Many tours involve lots of walking, standing, and time spent outdoors, so check the forecast before you head out.

Some tours are available only on certain days of the week (see the chart on the next two pages for specifics). For reservations and more information, call ☎ 407-WDW-TOUR (939-8687). Also check blog.touringplans.com for detailed reviews from our bloggers—just type the name of one of the tours listed here into the search box.

MULTIPARK TOURS

THE 7-HOUR **Backstage Magic** tour ($275) goes behind the scenes at all the WDW parks. Includes lunch; guests must be at least 16 years old to participate. Park admission is not required. The downside to this all-day tour is that you spend a lot of time in transit between the parks.

Disney's Holiday D-Lights (5 hours, $259) and **Disney's Yuletide Fantasy** (3 hours, $99) explore the myriad ways in which Walt Disney World transforms for the Christmas season. Neither tour requires park admission; guests must be at least age 16. Call ☎ 407-WDW-TOUR (939-8687) for 2017 tour dates; the holiday tours fill up quickly.

BEHIND *the* SCENES *at the* MAGIC KINGDOM

AS ITS NAME SUGGESTS, **Disney's Keys to the Kingdom** takes guests behind the scenes at the Magic Kingdom, providing a detailed look at the park's logistical, technical, and operational sides. Included are the parade-assembly area, the waste-treatment plant, and the utilidor network

BEHIND-THE-SCENES TOURS AT

TOUR (+ Minimum Age)	TOUR LENGTH	COST
MULTIPARK TOURS		
Backstage Magic (16 years old)	7 hours	$275
Disney's Holiday D-Lights (16 years old)	5 hours	$259
Disney's Yuletide Fantasy (16 years old)	3 hours	$99
THE MAGIC KINGDOM		
Disney's Family Magic Tour (no minimum age, but best for ages 4-10	1½-2 hrs.	$39
Disney's Keys to the Kingdom (16 years old)	4½-5 hrs.	$99
Disney's The Magic Behind Our Steam Trains (10 years old)	3 hours	$54
Disney's Wilderness Back Trail Adventure (*Fort Wilderness Campground*) | 16 years old and 100-250 lbs.	2 hours	$96
Pirates and Pals Fireworks Voyage (no minimum age)	2-3 hours	$72 ages 10+, $43 ages 3-9
Walt Disney: Marceline to Magic Kingdom Tour (12 years old)	3 hours	$49
EPCOT		
Behind the Seeds at Epcot (*Unofficial* Pick: Best Value) (no minimum age)	1 hour	$20 ages 10+, $16 ages 3-9
Dolphins in Depth (13 years old)	3 hours	$199
Epcot DiveQuest (10 years old)	3 hours	$179
Epcot Seas Aqua Tour (8 years old)	2½ hours	$145
The UnDISCOVERed Future World (16 years old)	4 hours	$69
World Showcase DestiNations Discovered (ages 16 and up)	5 hours	$109
DISNEY'S ANIMAL KINGDOM		
Starlight Safari at Disney's Animal Kingdom (8 years old)	1 hour	$75
Backstage Tales (12 years old)	3¾ hours	$90
Caring for the Giants (4 years old)	1 hour	$30
Savor the Savanna: Evening Safari Experience (*park admission required*) (8 years old)	3 hours	$169
Wild Africa Trek (*Unofficial* Pick: Best Family Tour) (8 years old and 48" tall)	3 hours	$189-$249
DISNEY'S HOLLYWOOD STUDIOS		
Star Wars Guided Tour (4 years old)	7 hours	$129
DISNEY'S CONTEMPORARY RESORT		
Highway in the Sky Dine Around Progressive Dinner (21+ to drink)	4 hours	$160

beneath the park. The program ($79 per person) includes lunch and runs about 4½–5 hours; children must be at least 16 years old.

Disney's The Magic Behind Our Steam Trains, a 3-hour tour for children ages 10 and up ($54 per person), takes a backstage look at the steam locomotives of the Walt Disney World Railroad. **Disney's Family Magic Tour** is an interactive romp through the park following clues in a

WALT DISNEY WORLD

FOCUS	DAYS AVAILABLE
Peeks behind the scenes at every Disney World park	M–F
Close-up look at Disney World holiday spectacles	Seasonal
Another look at holiday productions	Seasonal
Following clues in a sort of treasure hunt	Daily
Park's logistical, technical, and operational sides	Daily
Steam locomotives of the Walt Disney World Railroad	Daily
Segway romp on campground trails and paths	Tu–Sa
Cruise around Seven Seas Lagoon	Daily *(varies seasonally)*
Examination of Walt Disney's career and vision	Daily
Vegetable gardens in The Land	Daily
Visiting the dolphin-research facility at SeaBase in The Seas, plus 30 minutes of dolphin interaction	Tu–Sa
Swimming with the fish at SeaBase	Tu–Sa
Swimming in the main tank at SeaBase	Tu–Sa
The history of Epcot	Daily
Design of World Showcase pavilions, plus lunch	Daily, 9:30 and 10 a.m.
After-dark night-vision tour of lodge's savannas	Nightly, 10 p.m.
Observing how the animals are housed and cared for	Daily, usually 7:30 a.m.
Learn about Animal Kingdom's elephants	Daily, 10 a.m.–4:30 p.m.
Private safari followed by dinner at Jiko— The Cooking Place	Daily, 3:30 p.m.
Enhanced safari and adventure activities with meal	Daily
Take a wild guess!	M, W, F, Sa
Stops at three Disney resort hotels, ending with the *Happily Ever After* fireworks show at Disney's Contemporary Resort	Tu, F, Sa

sort of treasure hunt. The 1½- to 2-hour tour is offered daily for $39. **Walt Disney: Marceline to Magic Kingdom Tour** (3 hours, $35 ages 12 and up) interprets the Magic Kingdom as a "walking time line" of Disney's life (Marceline, Missouri, was his childhood hometown).

The Contemporary Resort's **Pirates and Pals Fireworks Voyage** (2–3 hours, $69 ages 10 and up; $41 ages 3–9) offers sailings with a unique view of the *Happily Ever After* fireworks from Seven Seas Lagoon; days vary seasonally but typically include Friday–Tuesday. Your guide, Patch, sings pirate songs and delights kids with Disney trivia. On select nights, the voyage also includes a viewing of the Floating Electrical Pageant.

Disney's Wilderness Back Trail Adventure ($95) is a 2-hour Segway romp on the trails and walking paths of Fort Wilderness Campground. Guests must be at least 16 years old and weigh 100–250 pounds.

The Contemporary Resort now offers a 4-hour progressive dinner called **Highway in the Sky Dine Around** ($160). You'll enjoy appetizers and cocktails at The Wave . . . of American Flavors and Polynesian Village Resort before taking the monorail to the Grand Floridian Resort for a selection of artisanal cheeses or charcuterie and the main course at Cítricos. The experience culminates back at the Contemporary with dessert and the *Happily Ever After* fireworks show.

BEHIND *the* SCENES *at* EPCOT

A TOUR CALLED **The UnDISCOVERed Future World** ($69, ages 16 and up) traces the history of Epcot, including Walt Disney's original concept. The tour takes guests to backstage areas and lasts a bit over 4 hours.

The hourlong **Behind the Seeds at Epcot** ($20 adults, $16 ages 3–9) tours the vegetable gardens and aquaculture farms in The Land. The quality of the experience—a cross between science lecture and Willy Wonka factory tour—depends heavily on the guide's presentation. Requires park admission and same-day reservations; make them on the lower level of The Land (next to the entrance to Soarin'). We think this is the best value among Disney's behind-the-scenes tours.

World Showcase DestiNations Discovered covers the design of World Showcase's pavilions, including their backstage areas. The tour is for guests ages 16 and up, costs $109, and includes lunch.

EPCOT DIVEQUEST

THE SOGGIEST BEHIND-THE-SCENES experience anywhere is **Epcot DiveQuest,** in which guests who are open water scuba–certified (ages 10 and up; kids ages 12 and younger must be accompanied by an adult) can swim with the fish at SeaBase, the exhibit-aquarium area of The Seas with Nemo & Friends Pavilion. Offered Tuesday–Saturday, at 4:30 and 5:30 p.m., each tour lasts about 3 hours, including a 40-minute dive. Cost is $179 per diver and includes all gear, a souvenir bag, and a dive-log stamp. Call ☎ 407-560-5590 for recorded information. Epcot admission is not required, but proof of dive certification is.

DOLPHINS IN DEPTH

THIS TOUR (AGES 13 AND UP) visits the dolphin-research facility at SeaBase. There you'll witness a training session, then wade into the water for a photo (but not a swim) with a dolphin. Cost for the 3-hour experience is $199; kids ages 13–18 must be accompanied by an adult; expectant mothers may not participate. Theme park admission is not required. Wet suits are provided. Only eight guests per day can participate; call ☎ 407-WDW-TOUR (939-8687) when you're ready to book.

For $229–$459 (tax included), you can visit SeaWorld's **Discovery Cove** and actually swim with a dolphin. Though the experience is only about 30 minutes long, the ticket entitles visitors to an entire day at Discovery Cove. For more information, see page 715.

EPCOT SEAS AQUA TOUR

THIS IS SORT OF a watered-down (ba-dump-bump) version of Epcot DiveQuest. The 2½-hour tour lets guests ages 8 and up swim with goggles, a mini–air tank, and a flotation vest in the main SeaBase tank for 30 minutes and explore backstage areas at The Seas with Nemo & Friends. It costs $145 and doesn't require separate park admission. Children under age 12 must be accompanied by an adult; children ages 12–17 must have a parent or guardian sign a waiver. Gear is included.

BEHIND *the* SCENES *at* DISNEY'S ANIMAL KINGDOM

IN THE 3¾-HOUR **Backstage Tales** tour, animal keepers and vets discuss conservation, animal care and behavior, and other topics. Limited to guests ages 12 and older, Backstage Tales costs $90. You'll see animal enclosures, feed bins, medical facilities, and labs, but not many animals.

Our pick for best family tour at Walt Disney World, the **Wild Africa Trek** (3 hours, $189–$249) takes groups of up to 12 on forest hiking trails, suspension bridges high above hippo and crocodile pools, and a private safari complete with a gourmet meal. Open to guests ages 8 and older. Extensive walking is required; guests must weigh 45–310 pounds and be at least 4 feet tall for the safety gear. A host of other warnings applies, so call Disney for details. Park admission is required.

The **Starlight Safari** is offered only to guests of Animal Kingdom Lodge & Villas (book through the concierge).

Caring for the Giants is a 1-hour tour led by an animal-care specialist, focusing on the care of the park's elephants. Tours take place daily between 10 a.m. and 4:30 p.m. Must be age 4 or older. Cost is $30 per person (tax included); park admission is required but not included.

BEHIND *the* SCENES *at* DISNEY'S HOLLYWOOD STUDIOS

THE 7-HOUR **Star Wars Guided Tour** includes a screening of *Star Wars: Path of the Jedi*; a reserved viewing area for *Star Wars: A Galaxy Far, Far Away*, the March of the First Order, and the *Star Wars: A Galactic Spectacular* nighttime fireworks; a Star Wars–inspired dinner at Backlot Express; and the *Star Wars: A Galactic Spectacular* Dessert Party. Children ages 4–12 receive guaranteed enrollment and participation in the *Jedi Training: Trials of the Temple* show. Guest also have VIP access to Star Tours—The Adventures Continue and Star Wars characters.

The tour costs $128.86 (tax included) for all ages and requires valid park admission. If you don't mind the astronomical price tag, call ☎ 407-WDW-PLAY (939-7529).

▌ VIP TOURS

WE CAN TELL BY THE BOOK you're reading that you're smart, and probably drop-dead gorgeous to boot. If you're also loaded and looking to avoid every possible line at Disney World while having most of your whims catered to, then a private VIP tour is what you want.

For $400–$600 per hour (depending on the season) and a 6-hour minimum, a Disney VIP host will pick you up at your resort, precheck your admission tickets, and whisk you and up to nine of your friends through a private entrance to a Disney theme park. Once in the park, your VIP guide will ensure that you wait as little as possible for whatever attractions you want to see (usually by taking you through the FastPass+ line, even if you don't have reservations) and make sure you get prime spots for viewing parades and fireworks. If you want to visit multiple parks, the VIP guide will drive you in a private car.

Unofficial Guide readers rave about the guides, who do everything from entertain the kids to regale the adults with obscure theme park trivia. They can also arrange meals.

One of our favorite people, travel goddess **Sue Pisaturo** of Small World Vacations, had this to say about her experience:

> *I'm usually the designated tour guide when we go to WDW. This time, I was so happy that no one asked me, "Where do we go next?" The convenience and stress-free touring were priceless.*

Tours can be booked between 3 and 90 days in advance by calling ☎ 407-560-4033. You must cancel at least 48 hours in advance to avoid a charge of 2 hours at the booked rate. To book one of the following three VIP tours, call ☎ 407-WDW-TOUR (939-8687).

The **Ultimate Day for Young Families–VIP Tour Experience** and **Ultimate Day of Thrills–VIP Experience** (7 hours, $299 per person) include rides on 12 attractions in the Magic Kingdom, Disney's Hollywood Studios, and Animal Kingdom, plus lunch at a Disney full-service restaurant. The Young Families tour features rides such as Dumbo and Toy Story Mania!, while the Thrills tour includes headliners such as Space Mountain and Tower of Terror. Transportation between parks is included, but park admission is not—you'll need the Park Hopper feature on your ticket. Annual Pass holders, Disney Vacation Club members, and Disney Visa Card holders get a 15% discount on Tuesday, Friday, and Sunday.

The **Ultimate Day VIP Tour at the Epcot International Food & Wine Festival** (6½ hours, $399 per person) takes places Thursdays and Sundays on select dates September–November (see page 53 for details). It includes Champagne and appetizers, a six-course tapas lunch, food and beverage tastings, rides on popular attractions such as Soarin' and Test Track, behind-the-scenes tours, VIP seating at one of the festival's Eat to the Beat concerts (featuring celebrity headliners such as Rick Springfield and Chaka Khan), and reserved seating at *IllumiNations*.

PART SIXTEEN

DISNEY SPRINGS, UNIVERSAL CITYWALK, SHOPPING, *and* NIGHTLIFE

VACATIONS AREN'T JUST THEME PARKS and attractions. It turns out many people want to shop, see live entertainment, or just let loose in the evening. This chapter is for you.

Both Walt Disney World and Universal Orlando have built huge outdoor mall complexes with restaurants, shopping, and theaters, so their hotel and theme park guests never need to spend money outside their borders. This chapter covers both locations, known as **Disney Springs** and **Universal CityWalk,** plus the best shopping in the Orlando area and nightlife options at both Walt Disney World and Universal.

DISNEY SPRINGS

THE AREA NOW KNOWN AS DISNEY SPRINGS has had a long history at Walt Disney World. Built in 1975 as Lake Buena Vista Shopping Village, a modest retail area, it is now one of the largest shopping and dining destinations in Orlando in or out of a theme park. Construction inside Disney Springs is largely complete, though road work to widen Buena Vista Drive will affect guests driving there from other areas on Walt Disney World property.

ARRIVING AND GETTING AROUND

BY CAR Guests driving themselves to Disney Springs will take Buena Vista Drive from Disney property; Hotel Plaza Boulevard from the Disney Springs resorts and FL 535; and directly from I-4. There are two parking garages and surface lots. The Lime garage offers access to The Landing, Town Center, and Marketplace areas of Disney Springs. The Orange garage is closest to the West Side, the AMC 16, and Planet Hollywood Observatory. There is no charge to park in either garage.

An LED display on each level of both garages indicates how many open spaces there are on each level. As rule, lower levels fill up first, with more open spaces available on each successive level up. The Lime garage can be reached from a westbound exit on I-4 and from Buena Vista Drive. The Orange garage entrance is from Buena Vista Drive.

Continued on page 750

Disney Springs

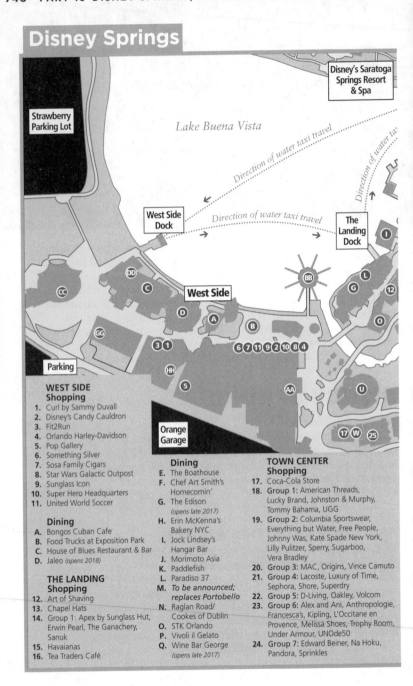

Disney's Saratoga Springs Resort & Spa

Strawberry Parking Lot

Lake Buena Vista

Direction of water taxi travel

Direction of water ta...

West Side Dock

Direction of water taxi travel

The Landing Dock

West Side

Parking

Orange Garage

WEST SIDE

Shopping

1. Curl by Sammy Duvall
2. Disney's Candy Cauldron
3. Fit2Run
4. Orlando Harley-Davidson
5. Pop Gallery
6. Something Silver
7. Sosa Family Cigars
8. Star Wars Galactic Outpost
9. Sunglass Icon
10. Super Hero Headquarters
11. United World Soccer

Dining

A. Bongos Cuban Cafe
B. Food Trucks at Exposition Park
C. House of Blues Restaurant & Bar
D. Jaleo *(opens 2018)*

THE LANDING

Shopping

12. Art of Shaving
13. Chapel Hats
14. Group 1: Apex by Sunglass Hut, Erwin Pearl, The Ganachery, Sanuk
15. Havaianas
16. Tea Traders Café

Dining

E. The Boathouse
F. Chef Art Smith's Homecomin'
G. The Edison *(opens late 2017)*
H. Erin McKenna's Bakery NYC
I. Jock Lindsey's Hangar Bar
J. Morimoto Asia
K. Paddlefish
L. Paradiso 37
M. *To be announced; replaces Portobello*
N. Raglan Road/ Cookes of Dublin
O. STK Orlando
P. Vivoli il Gelato
Q. Wine Bar George *(opens late 2017)*

TOWN CENTER

Shopping

17. Coca-Cola Store
18. Group 1: American Threads, Lucky Brand, Johnston & Murphy, Tommy Bahama, UGG
19. Group 2: Columbia Sportswear, Everything but Water, Free People, Johnny Was, Kate Spade New York, Lilly Pulitzer, Sperry, Sugarboo, Vera Bradley
20. Group 3: MAC, Origins, Vince Camuto
21. Group 4: Lacoste, Luxury of Time, Sephora, Shore, Superdry
22. Group 5: D-Living, Oakley, Volcom
23. Group 6: Alex and Ani, Anthropologie, Francesca's, Kipling, L'Occitane en Provence, Melissa Shoes, Trophy Room, Under Armour, UNOde50
24. Group 7: Edward Beiner, Na Hoku, Pandora, Sprinkles

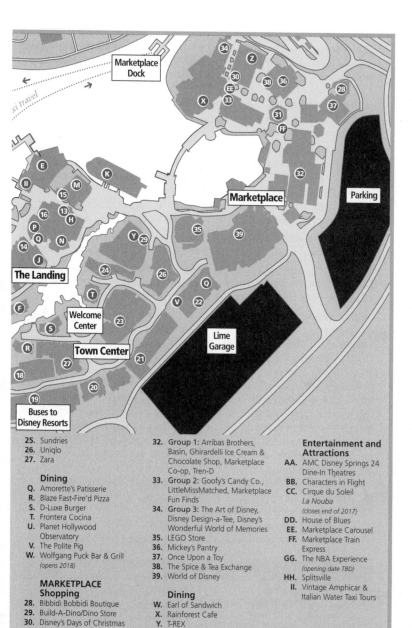

25. Sundries
26. Uniqlo
27. Zara

Dining

Q. Amorette's Patisserie
R. Blaze Fast-Fire'd Pizza
S. D-Luxe Burger
T. Frontera Cocina
U. Planet Hollywood Observatory
V. The Polite Pig
W. Wolfgang Puck Bar & Grill *(opens 2018)*

MARKETPLACE Shopping

28. Bibbidi Bobbidi Boutique
29. Build-A-Dino/Dino Store
30. Disney's Days of Christmas
31. Disney's Pin Traders

32. Group 1: Arribas Brothers, Basin, Ghirardelli Ice Cream & Chocolate Shop, Marketplace Co-op, Tren-D
33. Group 2: Goofy's Candy Co., LittleMissMatched, Marketplace Fun Finds
34. Group 3: The Art of Disney, Disney Design-a-Tee, Disney's Wonderful World of Memories
35. LEGO Store
36. Mickey's Pantry
37. Once Upon a Toy
38. The Spice & Tea Exchange
39. World of Disney

Dining

W. Earl of Sandwich
X. Rainforest Cafe
Y. T-REX
Z. Wolfgang Puck Express

Entertainment and Attractions

AA. AMC Disney Springs 24 Dine-In Theatres
BB. Characters in Flight
CC. Cirque du Soleil *La Nouba (closes end of 2017)*
DD. House of Blues
EE. Marketplace Carousel
FF. Marketplace Train Express
GG. The NBA Experience *(opening date TBD)*
HH. Splitsville
II. Vintage Amphicar & Italian Water Taxi Tours

Continued from page 747

Because the garages are immense, the idea is to find a parking space near an elevator bank. This is much more important than scoring a space on a lower level. When we park, we make a beeline to the top level, locate the elevators, and then park as close to them as possible. During the day, it's not unusual to find a space within 20–30 feet. Conditions change as the day progresses, but you're all but guaranteed to find the closest available space to the elevators on the top level. Valet parking is also available near the Orange garage for $20. All other parking is free.

BY DISNEY TRANSPORTATION All Disney resorts and theme parks offer bus transportation to Disney Springs. Some bus routes will include a pickup or drop-off at Typhoon Lagoon. The Disney bus area is centrally located close to the Orange garage.

Saratoga Springs, Old Key West, and the Port Orleans resorts offer boat transportation to the Disney Springs dock at The Landing.

BY TAXI/RIDE-SHARING SERVICE Drop-off and pickup is at the former Cirque du Soleil and the far end of the Marketplace.

BY FOOT Saratoga Springs has walking paths to the West Side and Marketplace. Guests at the Hotel Plaza Boulevard resorts can walk to Disney Springs via walkways and pedestrian bridges to avoid traffic.

DISNEY SPRINGS WATER TAXI Guests who don't wish to walk the length of Disney Springs can take a water taxi between points of interest. Docks are at the Marketplace close to Rainforest Café, The Landing close to Paradiso 37, and West Side close to House of Blues and the Strawberry parking lot.

Disney Springs is divided into four areas, each with its own theme. **Marketplace** is the most Disney and most kid-friendly, with World of Disney and many activities for children. It has a small carousel and mini–train rides for a nominal fee. A free splash area is great for cooling down, and free kid-oriented dance parties take place across from World of Disney in the amphitheater. The parties get kids out of the overwhelming flow of pedestrian traffic at night and look like a blast.

The Landing is the waterfront section of Disney Springs. Open, winding paths offer sweeping views of the water and Saratoga Springs as you walk between the Marketplace and West Side.

The newest area is Old Florida–style **Town Center,** which has most of the well-known retail of Disney Springs. Zara and Uniqlo are the

What's In and Out at Disney Springs

ENTERTAINMENT
- Cirque du Soleil La Nouba *(closes December 31, 2017)*
- DisneyQuest *(closed July 2017)*

RESTAURANTS
- The Edison *(opens late 2017)*
- Jaleo *(replaces Wolfgang Puck Grand Cafe; opens 2018)*
- Paddlefish *(formerly Fulton's Crab House)*
- Planet Hollywood Observatory *(reopened)*
- The Polite Pig
- To-be-named Italian eatery replacing Portobello *(opens late 2017)*
- Wine Bar George *(opens late 2017)*
- Wolfgang Puck Bar & Grill *(opens 2018)*

SHOPPING
- Coca-Cola Store

largest stores. If you've found yourself at Pirates of the Caribbean and thought, "What this place needs is an Orange Julius," you'll love shopping here.

With construction and updates to the other areas complete, Disney is now focusing on the **West Side.** Look for a new parking garage to come here in the next few years. Two of the West Side's largest pieces of real estate—Cirque du Soleil and DisneyQuest—closed in 2017 to make room for new tenants. **Splitsville** (page 398), an **AMC** multiplex, and **Starbucks** are the biggest draws.

DISNEY SPRINGS SHOPPING AT A GLANCE

Marketplace

BIBBIDI BOBBIDI BOUTIQUE (ALSO AT MAGIC KINGDOM) BBB, located at the far eastern end of the Disney Springs Marketplace next to Once Upon a Toy, is a salon for girls ages 3–12 that will give your princess hopeful a royal makeover, all of which includes so much hair spray that we suspect the place has an ozone hole hovering over it. Packages range from $60 to $200 plus tax and gratuity. While we may balk a bit that there's no PhD Princess or Med School Maiden package, we can't deny how popular Bibbidi Bobbidi Boutique is with both the kids getting the makeovers and their parents. Photo packages, a Knight Package (for the brother who has to sit around waiting for Susie to get her close-up), and other add-ons are available for an extra charge.

unofficial **TIP**
At **Ghirardelli Soda Fountain & Chocolate Shop,** you can smell the chocolate when you walk in, and most of the time a cast member is on hand to dole out free samples. Chocolate souvenirs abound, but treat yourself to a "world famous" sundae topped with the decadent hot fudge made daily at the shop. The line for ice cream often winds out the door—it's that good.

BBB can be reserved up to 180 days in advance (190 days for Disney resort guests); call ☎ 407-WDW-STYLE (939-7893) for information or reservations. Allow 30 minutes for the whole makeover.

DISNEY'S DAYS OF CHRISTMAS This shop is just plain fun, with hundreds of holiday decorations, from ornaments to stockings to stuffed animals wearing their Christmas best. We especially like the station for ornament personalization. There is a section dedicated to *The Nightmare Before Christmas.*

GOOFY'S CANDY CO. An interactive show kitchen with lots of sweets. Enjoy create-your-own pretzel rods, marshmallows, and candy apples.

LEGO IMAGINATION CENTER This is an ideal rest stop for parents, and you don't even have to go inside the store. A hands-on outdoor play area has bins of Legos that the kids can go crazy with while Mom and Dad take a break. Inside is all the latest Lego paraphernalia. Photo ops with life-size Disney characters surround the shop.

MARKETPLACE CO-OP The Co-op is loved among Disney fans for its six pop-up-style retail experiences within one shop. Areas include **Cherry Tree Lane** (character-themed women's clothes and accessories), **Disney Centerpiece** (home and kitchen items), **D-Tech on Demand** (custom electronics accessories), **Twenty Eight & Main** (men's goods), **WonderGround Gallery** (creative Disney-inspired original art), and **Disney TAG,** which features travel accessories with a retro and Disney touch.

ONCE UPON A TOY This is the place to find toy sets and a huge selection of plush; it's also the best place for books, video games, and other media. All the Disney franchises, from the Pixar titles to Marvel and Star Wars, are well represented here. We also appreciate that Once Upon a Toy is far less crowded than World of Disney.

TREN-D A fun, hip, urban-inspired boutique for women, with fashion apparel and accessories, plus exclusive items from cutting-edge designers and Disney merchandise you won't find anywhere else.

WORLD OF DISNEY With the largest selection of Disney merchandise on-site or anywhere else, World of Disney can get oppressively crowded at night. It has a little bit of everything, including a huge section devoted to princess wear (you can't miss it—it's very pink).

Town Center

AMORETTE'S PATISSERIE Beautiful cakes and pastries, Disney character–themed cakes, large and small, that you won't see anywhere else, and Champagne by the glass. Amorette's will deliver a cake to your Disney Springs restaurant for special occasions with 72 hours notice. *Note:* They don't deliver outside of Disney Springs.

COCA-COLA STORE Not a "best of" unless you're just really obsessed with Coke, but the roof deck does have a bar and views that overlook Disney Springs.

D-LIVING One of the few Disney-run shops in Town Center. It sells Disney home decor, most of which can be found elsewhere on the property.

KATE SPADE What sets this location apart from the one at your local mall is that it often has Disney-themed bags and accessories you can otherwise find only online.

LILLY PULITZER Bright, fun prints for the country club and sorority sets. Sadly, there are no Disney–Lilly exclusives here—a missed opportunity if you ask us.

MICKEY'S PANTRY/THE SPICE AND TEA EXCHANGE Recently remodeled, Mickey's Pantry now carries more flavored salts and sugars, teas, and spice mixes, and less melamine dishware. You can also purchase wines by the bottle and cookbooks. It is an unexpected surprise.

PANDORA The jewelry retailer has an agreement with Walt Disney World that includes another shop on Main Street, U.S.A., and sponsorship of the evening fireworks at Magic Kingdom. Many Disney-exclusive charms sell out quickly.

SUPERDRY Fun casual wear for teens and young adults. We can't put our finger on why we like Superdry, but we do.

TOMMY BAHAMA One of the few shops at Disney Springs with a decent selection of casual menswear. Also has a nice selection of swimwear for both men and women.

TROPHY ROOM Dedicated to all things Michael Jordan, including the eponymous Nike trainers. You can get a preview of the selection or shop online at trophyroomstore.com.

UNIQLO Fast fashion along with a nice selection of exclusive Disney apparel. Uniqlo is handy if you need to buy basics such as socks, underwear, and T-shirts.

VERA BRADLEY The ubiquitous quilted bags with a fanatical following. You'll find both Disney-exclusive and mainline prints here.

The Landing

THE ART OF SHAVING Sells shaving gear and also offers men's barber and shaving services, including a $50 haircut. Let us know if you try it.

THE GANACHERY Exquisite handmade chocolates in gourmet flavor combinations. This is a Disney-run shop. The candy may be more pricey than you're expecting, but the quality is solid. Makes a nice late-night treat in your hotel room.

TEA TRADERS CAFE BY JOFFREY'S You can purchase leaves to take home or enjoy a hot or cold tea at the counter. Very pleasant and less hectic than Starbucks for your beverage needs.

You'll also find a variety of kiosks selling everything from wind chimes to yo-yos as you walk through The Landing, including **Filthy Rich,** specializing in jewelry and accessories inspired by celebrities past and present.

Disney Springs West Side

DISNEY'S CANDY CAULDRON Watch as gooey treats are made in the open kitchen. Dipped candy apples (as befits the Snow White–Evil Queen theme) are the specialty of the house. There is also a decent selection of bulk candies.

FIT2RUN Running gear and runDisney merchandise.

SOMETHING SILVER Specializes in designer jewelry.

SOSA FAMILY CIGARS They hand-roll 'em and feature premium imports, including Arturo Fuente, Cuesta-Rey, Diamond Crown, La Gloria Cubana, Macanudo, Padrón, Partagas, Puros Indios, and Sosa. A walk-in humidor stores the top brands.

STAR WARS GALACTIC OUTPOST A large selection of Star Wars souvenirs, from T-shirts to Stormtrooper helmets. See page 761 for more on Star Wars swag.

SUPERHERO HEADQUARTERS This is the best place on Disney property to find Marvel merchandise. Through the wonders of contracts, Universal also has a great selection of Marvel items. We'll leave the details to the lawyers and just enjoy the shopping.

UNITED WORLD SOCCER Jerseys and sporting goods from your favorite football clubs. Fans can also find Orlando City (the local team) merchandise here.

NIGHTLIFE AT DISNEY SPRINGS

DISNEY SPRINGS IS A POPULAR destination after dark for folks who aren't ready to be in for the night but don't want to burn park admission for just a few hours in the evening. You'll find street entertainment, including singers, musicians, and performance artists spread throughout Disney Springs (it sometimes feels like they're spaced such that as soon as one is out of earshot, you can hear the next one). There's even more entertainment at many of the restaurants, including bands and singers at **Splitsville** (page 398) and **House of Blues** (page 381) and music and Irish dancers at **Raglan Road** (page 393).

Some of our favorite places to grab a drink are at Disney Springs. The aforementioned Raglan Road has multiple bars and a fantastic menu of appetizers. Splitsville offers a nice selection munchies and a decent (if largely premixed) cocktail menu. The Indiana Jones–themed **Jock Lindsey's Hangar Bar** (page 383) is a highly themed lounge with a thoughtful menu and indoor and waterside seating. **Morimoto Asia** (page 387) and **The Boathouse** (page 366) both have bars worth a visit. Opening in late 2017, **The Edison** (page 359) will bring cabaret and cocktails in an upscale atmosphere to Disney Springs.

TAKE IT ON THE RUN, BABY

FOR AN EVENING OF DRINKING AND STROLLING, Disney Springs has you covered. Starting with the **AmphiBar** outside the entrance to **The Boathouse,** the restaurants quickly figured out there was a real market for cocktails to go. Find Guinness outside Raglan Road and margaritas at **Frontera Cocina** and **Dockside Margaritas.**

UNIVERSAL CITYWALK

EVERY GUEST WHO DRIVES TO UNIVERSAL ORLANDO enters through Universal CityWalk, a complex of nightlife, retail, and dining establishments that caters to visitors and locals alike. On weekends, CityWalk draws far more locals than Disney Springs and, with its concentration of nightclubs, a much younger crowd. CityWalk also features a fantastically themed minigolf course, **Hollywood Drive-In Golf** (see page 773 in Part Seventeen, Recreation, Sports, and Spas), and a 20-screen **AMC Universal Cineplex.**

While CityWalk doesn't charge admission, visitors do need to pay for parking (see Part 13, page 668, for more information). Also, if you want to visit the nightclubs, note that you'll have to pay a cover charge in the evenings.

CITYWALK DINING

CITYWALK HAS DINING OPTIONS that range from fast food to upscale, with choices for families and serious foodies alike. We're wild about many of the new dining venues that have opened at CityWalk since mid-2014. Our favorites, including **Vivo Italian Kitchen** and **Antojitos,** serve delicious meals at a price point that would give a Disney stockholder heart palpitations.

A 2017 addition, **The Toothsome Chocolate Emporium and Savory Feast Kitchen,** serves outrageous ice cream and chocolate concoctions as well as steak, seafood, and all-day brunch. It'll delight your kids; plus, it has possibly the longest name of any Orlando restaurant.

Read more about CityWalk restaurants in Part Four, Dining in and around Walt Disney World, on pages 308–314.

CITYWALK SHOPPING

CITYWALK ISN'T AS RETAIL-HEAVY as Disney Springs, but you'll still find some interesting places to drop your dough.

ELEMENT Skateboarding gear and apparel.

FOSSIL Watches, accessories, and sunglasses.

FRESH PRODUCE Resort-casual clothing and accessories for women.

HART & HUNTINGTON TATTOO For guests with poor impulse control (or really great artistic vision), this outpost of the famous tattoo company provides the opportunity to make your vacation memories permanent—*really* permanent.

THE ISLAND CLOTHING STORE Shop here for upscale men's and women's clothing and accessories. (This is one of the few outlets in CityWalk that caters to men.) Brands include Tommy Bahama and Robert Graham. The Island shares space with **Quiet Flight Surf Shop,** which features more-casual clothes and sunglasses from surf and skate brands like Quiksilver and Billabong.

P!Q Sells a variety of gifts and pop-culture collectibles at a range of price points. Its selection reminds us of a slightly more tasteful gift area at your local Urban Outfitters.

QUIET FLIGHT SURF SHOP Surfboards, skateboards, and merchandise from Billabong, Quicksilver, Oakley, Volcom, Reef, Nixon, Von Zipper, Hurley, Rip Curl, and Roxy.

UNIVERSAL STUDIOS STORE A variety of theme-park merchandise.

CITYWALK NIGHTLIFE

THE FOLLOWING NIGHTCLUB VENUES are mostly located along the elevated, curving pathway that sits behind and above CityWalk's central plaza. At most of these venues, you must be 21 or older (passport or photo ID required) to enter after 9 p.m. Pick up a CityWalk City Guide brochure from the concierge stand or Guest Services for a monthly listing of live performances and drink specials.

Bob Marley—A Tribute to Freedom

What it is Reggae restaurant and club. **Hours** Daily, 4 p.m.–2 a.m. **Cuisine** Jamaican-influenced appetizers and main courses. **Entertainment** Live reggae bands and a DJ hold court in the outdoor gazebo every night. **Cover** $7 after 9 p.m. nightly (more for special acts).

COMMENTS This club is a re-creation of Marley's home in Kingston, Jamaica and contains a lot of interesting Marley memorabilia. The open-air courtyard is the center of action. Sunday is Ladies' Night, with no cover charge for women before midnight and drink specials. Island Sounds Wednesdays also feature free cover for ladies all night long, and drink specials 9 p.m.–2 a.m.

CityWalk's Rising Star

What it is Karaoke club with live band and backup singers Tuesday–Saturday (Sunday–Monday, sing to recorded tracks with live backup singers). **Hours** Nightly, 8 p.m.–2 a.m. **Cuisine** Red Oven pizza delivery. **Entertainment** Karaoke. **Cover** $7 (no extra charge to sing).

COMMENTS With live musicians backing you up, you can pretend that you've hit the big time at this opulent karaoke, which started life as CityWalk's jazz club. The song list is rather short, with only a little more than 200 options instead of the thousands you may be used to back home. Even so, this is an extremely popular spot; be sure to put your selections in as early in the evening as possible if you want to get onstage. While waiting your turn, you can get your courage up with a supersweet specialty cocktail. Guests ages 18 and older are welcome Sunday–Thursday, but the club is restricted to ages 21+ on Friday and Saturday.

The Groove

What it is High-tech disco. **Hours** Nightly, 9 p.m.–2 a.m. **Cuisine** No food. **Entertainment** DJ plays dance tunes; sometimes there are live bands. **Cover** $7.

COMMENTS This *très chic* club designed to look like an old theater in the midst of restoration features seven bars and several themed cubbyholes (the ultramodern Blue Room, laid-back Green Room, and bordello-like Red Room) for getting away from the thundering sound system. Dancers are barraged with strobes, lasers, and heaven knows what else. VIP reserved tables with premium bottle service are available for those with money and liver cells to burn; call ☎ 407-224-2166 to book your party. Attire is casual chic with no hats or tank tops permitted for men.

Jimmy Buffett's Margaritaville

What it is Key West–themed restaurant and club. **Hours** Daily, 11 a.m.–2 a.m. **Cuisine** Caribbean, Florida fusion, and American. **Entertainment** Live rock and island-style music. **Cover** $7 after 10 p.m.

COMMENTS Jimmy's is a big place with three bars that turns into a nightclub after 10 p.m. Jimmy Buffett covers are popular (no surprise), as are island music and light rock. If you eat dinner here, you'll probably want to find another vantage point when the band cranks up on the main stage around 9 p.m. There's always an acoustic guitarist strumming on the Porch of Indecision from 5 p.m. daily. If you are already inside the restaurant eating dinner before the cover charge kicks in, you won't be kicked out when the band kicks off.

Pat O'Brien's Orlando

What it is Dueling pianos sing-along club and restaurant. **Hours** Daily, 4 p.m.–2 a.m. **Cuisine** Cajun/Creole. **Entertainment** Dueling pianos and sing-alongs. **Cover** $7 after 9 p.m. for piano bar only.

COMMENTS A clone of the famous New Orleans club of the same name. A solo pianist starts playing a little after 5 p.m., and he or she is joined by a second pianist starting around 9 p.m. These are some of the most talented singing musicians in town and will happily handle nearly any request you throw at them (even—gasp!—Disney tunes) as long as you write it on a generous gratuity. You can dine in the courtyard or on the terrace without paying a cover.

The Red Coconut Club

What it is Modern lounge and nightclub. **Hours** Monday–Saturday, 7 p.m.–2 a.m.; Sunday, 8 p.m.–2 a.m. **Cuisine** Appetizers; Red Oven pizza delivery after 10 p.m. **Entertainment** Lounging and dancing. **Cover** $7 after 9 p.m.

COMMENTS This nightspot is billed as a nightclub and ultralounge (advertising speak for "hip place to be seen"). The eclectic mix of decor—part 1950s, part tiki—and three bars on two levels would make it a great latter-day hangout for the Rat Pack, if Frank and Dean happened to be resurrected in Orlando. There is a dance floor, and the bar serves signature martinis and mojitos. An evening here can quickly add up, with VIP bottle service starting at $100; a daily happy hour from 7 p.m. to 9 p.m. brings the drink and appetizer prices down to more reasonable levels. Thursday is Latin Ladies Night with DJ Leony; there's no cover for women.

SHOPPING *in the* THEME PARKS *and* ORLANDO

WE ALMOST TITLED THIS SECTION "Exit Through the Gift Shop," but that would have been a cliché (and Banksy beat us to it). Retail is a huge revenue source for both Disney and Universal. If you enjoy shopping, we recommend setting aside some time and money to do so. And even if you don't enjoy it, you may be traveling with someone who does, so keep the tips below in mind as you exit through . . . well, you know.

> ✳ *unofficial* **TIP**
> In 2015, Walt Disney World ceased selling any souvenir guns (from Frontierland muskets to Buzz Lightyear laser blasters) in the parks. Swords (Pirates of the Caribbean) and light sabers (an elegant weapon for a more civilized age) are still OK.

SHOPPING AT DISNEY WORLD

Each theme park has at least one major retail space, several minor ones, and space attached to most attractions. While we occasionally bemoan the homogenization of the merchandise selection, this does mean that if something catches your eye, you'll most likely see it again. Ditto for sale prices. Pricing is consistent throughout the resorts, and an item on sale in one location will be the same price at all locations.

See the next page for a quick-reference guide to which theme park shops carry the stuff you're looking for.

EPCOT SHOPPING Retail is a huge part of the World Showcase experience at Epcot, much more so than at the other theme parks. This is one of the few times on your vacation that you won't be able to say "well, I'll see it again later" if something catches your eye. With a selection that ranges from affordable trinkets to Mikimoto pearl-and-diamond earrings, the shops in World Showcase have something for everyone. Walking clockwise around World Showcase, you'll find:

★ **MEXICO** Probably the most immersive shopping experience in World Showcase, **Plaza de los Amigos** is a re-creation of a Mexican shopping village at dusk. You'll find all manner of sombreros, Day of the Dead items, Oaxacan carved wooden animals, and blankets. Along the side of the shopping area is **La Princesa Cristal,** with crystal jewelry and trinkets, and another shop with leather items, women's dresses and blouses, and other accessories. If you need a break from shopping, the **San Angel Inn Restaurante** (page 396) and *Unofficial* favorite watering hole **La Cava del Tequila** (page 338) are just off the shopping area.

MAGIC KINGDOM SHOPPING SAMPLER	
I WANT . . .	**FIND IT AT . . .**
• One-stop shopping	• **The Emporium,** Main Street
• Candy, pastries, fudge	• **Main Street Confectionery,** Main Street • **Big Top Treats,** Fantasyland
• Disney art and collectibles	• **The Art of Disney,** Main Street
• Holiday decor	• **Olde Christmas Shoppe,** Liberty Square
• Memory cards and batteries	• **Box Office Gifts,** Main Street
• Personalized mouse ears	• **The Chapeau,** Main Street • **Fantasy Faire,** Fantasyland
• Princess wear	• **The Emporium,** Main Street • **Castle Couture,** Fantasyland
• Tech gifts	• **Space Mountain Gift Shop,** Tomorrowland
• Women's jewelry, handbags, accessories	• **Main Street Jewelers** (has a **Pandora** shop)

EPCOT SHOPPING SAMPLER	
I WANT . . .	**FIND IT AT . . .**
• One-stop shopping	• **MouseGear,** Future World
• Disney art and collectibles	• **The Art of Disney,** Future World
• Disney comics and books	• **ImageWorks,** Imagination! Pavilion
• Eco-friendly gifts	• **Outpost,** World Showcase
• Kitchen supplies and decor	• **Port of Entry,** World Showcase
• Memory cards and batteries	• **Camera Center,** Future World
• Personalized mouse ears	• **MouseGear,** Future World
• Princess-wear	• **The Puffin's Roost,** Norway Pavilion
• Tech gifts	• **MouseGear** and **Camera Center,** • **Future World**

★ **NORWAY The Puffin's Roost** is a series of small shopping galleries with popular imports such as trolls (from $15) and wooden Christmas ornaments ($4 and up). Other hard-to-find imports include Scandinavian foods and candies, Laila perfume and body lotion, and Helly Hansen and Dale of Norway clothing, including thick woolen sweaters. The Puffin's Roost is home to all things Frozen.

★ **CHINA** This pavilion features one of our favorite shops, piled with such imports as real silk kimonos, cloisonné, and thick silk rugs. **House of Good Fortune** is more like a rambling department store than a shop. You'll find everything here, from silk fans to $4,000 jade sculptures to antique furniture. The silk dresses and robes are competitively priced in the $100 range. Darling handbags are $10 and up, and silk ties are around $20. We always admire the handwoven pure-silk carpets, starting around $300 for a 2-foot rug and topping out around $2,500 for a 4 x 8–foot rug. The prices are comparable to what you'd pay in a retail shop—if you could find one that imports carpets like these.

Village Traders, a shop between China and Germany, sells African woodcarvings that are as unusual as they come. Another specialty here is beautiful bead jewelry, crafted in Uganda from repurposed Disney paper products such as old handout guides.

DISNEY'S ANIMAL KINGDOM SHOPPING SAMPLER	
I WANT . . .	**FIND IT AT . . .**
• One-stop shopping	• **Disney Outfitters,** Discovery Island
• African souvenirs	• **Mombasa Marketplace,** Harambe, Africa
• Dinosaur kitsch and toys	• **Chester and Hester's Dinosaur Treasures,** DinoLand U.S.A.
• Memory cards and batteries	• **Island Mercantile,** Discovery Island
• Personalized mouse ears	• **Island Mercantile,** Discovery Island
• African wines, cookbooks, and Flame Tree barbecue sauce	• **Zuri's Sweets Shop,** Africa
• My own shoulder-top banshee or glowing Pandora merch	• **Windtraders,** Pandora: Land of Avatar

DISNEY'S HOLLYWOOD STUDIOS SHOPPING SAMPLER	
I WANT . . .	**FIND IT AT . . .**
• One-stop shopping	• **Mickey's of Hollywood,** Hollywood Blvd.
• Candy, pastries, fudge	• **Beverly Sunset,** Hollywood and Sunset
• Holiday decor	• **It's a Wonderful Shop,** Streets of America
• Memory cards and batteries, tech gifts	• **The Darkroom,** Hollywood Blvd.
• Personalized mouse ears	• **Adrian and Edith's Head to Toe,** Hollywood Blvd.
• Princess wear	• **Legends of Hollywood,** Sunset Blvd.
• Retro men's clothing and gifts	• **Keystone Clothiers,** Hollywood Blvd
• Women's jewelry, handbags, accessories	• **Keystone Clothiers,** Hollywood Blvd

★ **GERMANY** Shops interconnect on both sides of the cobblestoned central plaza and purvey an impressive collection of imports. Tiny **Das Kaufhaus** stocks a nice selection of Adidas sportswear. Next door is **Volkskunst,** where the walls are covered with Schneider cuckoo clocks and the shelves are stocked with limited-edition steins and glassware. Next is **Der Teddybär,** featuring Engel-Puppen dolls and Steiff plush toys, among other delights for kids. Across the plaza, **Kunstarbeit in Kristall** carries a fabulous collection of Swarovski crystal, including pins, glassware, and Arribas Brothers collectibles (check out the limited-edition $37,500 replica of Cinderella's Castle, blinged out with more than 20,000 Swarovski crystals). Next is the **Weinkeller,** with nearly 300 varieties of German wine. Step through the door to **Die Weihnachts Ecke,** where Christmas ornaments and handmade nutcrackers are on display year-round. Anyone with a sweet tooth will go crazy just smelling the most delicious addition to Germany's lineup, **Karamell-Küche.** Treats are made in-house with Werther's Original caramel, from caramel apples to cookies and candies made or drizzled with caramel. You'll also find an impressive selection of Werther's Original candies.

★ **ITALY Il Bel Cristallo** showcases Puma sportswear, Bulgari and Emilio Pucci fragrances, Murano figurines, elaborate Venetian masks, and a small selection of Christmas decorations in the back room.

TIPS FOR AVOIDING BUYER'S REMORSE

1. Know ahead of time how much things cost. Many theme park items are available at disneystore.com.

2. Be specific. Disney collecting can spiral out of control if you don't narrow your focus. Pick a character or movie you love, and stick to that.

3. Don't buy dated merchandise. That Walt Disney World 2018 T-shirt you buy to commemorate your vacation is going to look awfully silly on January 1, 2019. There's a reason this stuff is the number-one seller at Disney outlets.

4. The local big box stores will have a selection of low-priced Disney and Universal souvenirs. Look for them at the fronts of the stores.

5. Don't fall for "limited editions." If they make 2,000 of something, is it really limited?

6. Wait. Don't make your purchases until you've been to more than one shop.

7. Consider comestibles as souvenirs. There's no buyer's remorse if you can consume the evidence.

8. Some of the best things in life are free. Consider our favorite freebies at Walt Disney World (see next page), and skip the cash register.

★ **THE AMERICAN ADVENTURE Heritage Manor Gifts** carries patriotic gifts with a twist, such as American-made candy and regional souvenirs.

★ **JAPAN** A branch of Japan's 300-year-old **Mitsukoshi Department Store** stretches along one entire side of the pavilion. Kid-friendly merchandise (Hello Kitty, Naruto, and Yu-Gi-Oh!) fills the front, with kimonos, slippers, handbags, and lots more at the back. Mitsukoshi's expanded culinary display includes a sake-tasting bar, along with chopsticks, pretty rice bowls, a large variety of teas and teapots, and imported snacks. Mitsukoshi is currently undergoing an expansion. Its selection of anime is greatly increased. The room of Mikimoto jewelry is closed during construction. Tourists line up for an oyster guaranteed to have a pearl in its shell (pearls are polished for you by the salesperson).

★ **MOROCCO** Several shops wend through this pavilion: **Tangier Traders** sells traditional Moroccan clothing, shoes, and fezzes; **The Brass Bazaar** features brass, of course, and ceramic and wooden kitchenware (not dishwasher safe); and **Casablanca Carpets** offers a wide variety of Moroccan rugs, as well as decorative pieces such as abstract-shaped lamps, sequined pillows, and incense holders.

★ **FRANCE** The courtyard at the France pavilion has great shopping opportunities. A dedicated Guerlain shop, **La Signature,** offers cosmetics and fragrances from the French house. **Plume et Palette** has more fragrances, cosmetics, and women's accessories from Dior, Kenzo, and Thierry Mugler, to name a few. You can find wines and kitchen goods, including a Champagne tasting counter at **Les Vins de France** and **L'Esprit de la Provence,** which are connecting shops. And finally, at the back of the pavilion, **Souvenirs de France** sells a bit of everything French, from berets and Eiffel tower models to T-shirts and language books.

★ **UNITED KINGDOM** A handful of interesting imports are scattered throughout a half dozen small shops. **The Toy Soldier** stocks costumes, books, and plush toys featuring English characters from favorite films and television shows, such as *Dr. Who* and *Downton Abbey,* as well as British rock 'n' roll–themed items, including Beatles merchandise.

You'll find plenty of Alice in Wonderland, Peter Pan, and Winnie the Pooh merchandise, too. Stop at **The Crown & Crest** to look up your family name in the coat-of-arms book, and the shop will create your family's insignia in a beautiful frame of your choice. At the adjacent **Sportsman's Shoppe,** you'll find plenty of football (soccer) apparel, balls, and books.

Across the street, you'll find **The Queen's Table,** a gift shop with UK-themed clothing, glassware, and more. **Lords and Ladies,** a quaint store, offers lotions, soaps, scarves, jewelry, and perfume from the United Kingdom. **The Tea Caddy** stocks Twinings tea, biscuits, and candy.

★ **CANADA** There's not much shopping here, but **Northwest Mercantile** has a wide selection of merchandise, including NHL jerseys, T-shirts, sweatshirts, aprons, and pajamas. Bottles of ice wine and maple syrup make nice souvenirs for foodies.

Our Favorite Free Souvenirs from Walt Disney World

CELEBRATION BUTTONS Just married? Just graduated? Just happy to be nominated? There's a button for that.

CHOCOLATE Ghirardelli at Disney Springs gives out free samples.

KIDCOT FUN STOP CRAFTS Sometimes the best souvenir is the one you make yourself (or at least it's a good line to tell your kids).

PHOTOS Ask one of the Memory Maker photographers to take a photo with your camera.

BIRTHDAY TREATS Be sure to mention any special occasions you're celebrating when you check in for your meal at a full-service restaurant. You may get a surprise dessert.

SORCERERS OF THE MAGIC KINGDOM CARDS You can get one pack per day per player at the Magic Kingdom; special cards (also free) are given out during some events, such as the Halloween and Christmas parties.

STICKERS Cast members give out so many of these, we're afraid there might be an adhesive shortage.

TRANSPORTATION TRADING CARDS Did you know that monorail and bus drivers have trading cards to give out?

TOILETRIES We may or may not have hoards of Disney resort shampoos, bath gels, and soaps in our own homes.

The Force Is Strong . . . on Your Wallet

Since before the release of *Star Wars: The Force Awakens* in 2015, Walt Disney World has seen a huge increase in the amount of space dedicated to Star Wars merchandise. The difference was so noticeable that on one trip we tried to find a place that didn't sell the stuff. We were unsuccessful and, needless to say, perplexed when we located Star Wars souvenirs in both Animal Kingdom and Fantasyland. There are four places we recommend any fan check for memorabilia: **Tatooine Traders** and **Star Wars Launch Bay** at Hollywood Studios, and **Once Upon a Toy** and **Galactic Outpost** in Disney Springs. Aside from the Disney–Star Wars mash-ups (one of our favorites is the C3PO mouse-ears hats), customizable items make great gifts.

More Tips for Disney Shopping

Don't want to carry your stuff around? If you're staying at a Disney hotel, you can have your packages delivered to your resort from any of the four Disney parks. Packages will be delivered to the gift shop by noon the following day, so this service is unavailable if you're checking out of your room the same day. Same-day pickup inside the theme parks is available. For a nominal charge, you can ship items to your home.

A New Brunswick, Canada, reader spread the news:

> *I can't help but wonder how well known the parks' delivery services are. In Epcot I overheard two shoppers discussing whether they should buy a large pint glass; a major point of discussion was, "How would we get it home?" I chimed in to tell them all about Disney's Package Pick-Up service.*

If you realize on your flight home that you forgot to buy mouse ears for your niece, don't worry. The **Disney Store** online (disneystore .com) has a dedicated section of parks merchandise.

SHOPPING OUTSIDE DISNEY WORLD

Upscale Shopping

The Mall at Millenia is anchored by **Bloomingdale's, Macy's,** and **Neiman Marcus.** You'll find designer boutiques, such as **Burberry, Chanel, Gucci, Louis Vuitton, Salvatore Ferragamo,** and **Yves Saint Laurent,** as well. Millenia also has the closest **Apple Store** to Universal or Walt Disney World. It isn't entirely high-end, however, with fast-fashion staples such as **H&M** and **Forever 21,** as well as the usual suspects such as **Gap, Victoria's Secret,** and **J.Crew.** Visit mallatmillenia.com for a directory.

Midscale Shopping

The Florida Mall is home to **Dillard's, JC Penney, Macy's,** and **Sears.** Apart from the anchors and high-end designer shops, it has much the same selection as Millenia. Visit simon.com/mall/the-florida-mall.

Outlet Shopping

If you think the crowds at the parks can be overwhelming, avoid the two **Orlando Premium Outlets** (premiumoutlets.com/orlando) at International Drive and Vineland Avenue. Tourists arrive here by the busload, and the experience will leave you questioning everything from consumer culture to your own judgment in dropping by. For the theme park visitor, the only redeeming aspect of these two shopping malls is the **Disney Character Warehouse** (there are locations at both outlets).

Disney Shopping Outside of Walt Disney World

The Disney outlet at Vineland is about twice the size of the location on I-Drive. To get an idea of the stuff you'll find there, check out the TouringPlans blog (tinyurl.com/disoutlet), in which Derek Burgan makes a monthly journey to get the scoop on what Disney made too much of.

Fans who really want to take home a piece of their vacation should head to **TD Collectibles** (1218 Winter Garden Vineland Road, Suite 112; ☎ 407-347-0670; tdcollectibles.net) for one-of-a-kind items, including costumes, props, and local art. Hours are Tuesday–Friday, 10 a.m.–5 p.m., and Saturday, 10 a.m.–2 p.m. **Theme Park Connection** has closed its retail locations and is now online only (themepark connection.com); find everything from old signage to old ride vehicles.

Orlando International Airport has two Disney shops, one at each terminal, for purchases you need to make on the way home. These are fairly large and well themed for airport shops and are run by Disney. They're good spots to kill time if you arrive early for your flight.

SHOPPING AT UNIVERSAL ORLANDO

UNIVERSAL WASN'T ALWAYS KNOWN for souvenirs . . . but then Harry Potter happened. If your young Muggles need to gear up for their time at Hogwarts, you're in the right place. What we love about the shopping experience in The Wizarding World of Harry Potter is how well integrated it is with the rest of the land; it's almost an attraction in itself.

Incredibly popular in The Wizarding World are the $53 interactive wands that trigger special effects throughout both Diagon Alley and Hogsmeade Village. Because of the price, you may wonder if their powers extend beyond Universal, but alas, their only magic is making money disappear from your wallet.

If Harry Potter isn't your thing, Universal offers other interesting shopping opportunities in its parks. Our favorites are the **Kwik-E-Mart** in Springfield, for *Simpsons* memorabilia, and the new ultra-*kawaii* **Hello Kitty** shop on Hollywood Boulevard. **Marvel Comics** fans have a great selection with an actual comic book shop on Marvel Super Hero Island in Islands of Adventure, and **DC Comics** fans will enjoy the surprising large selection at the quite-difficult-to-find **Cyber Image,** which is the shop at the exit of the Terminator attraction.

There is also a Universal gift shop at **Orlando International Airport** for any last-minute gift needs.

> *un*official **TIP**
> The merchandise locations inside both Wizarding World areas are very immersive but also tend to be both crowded and dark. If you find the shopping experience there too much, rest assured that you can purchase many Harry Potter items at the other Universal shops and in your Universal resort hotel gift shop.

ENTERTAINMENT *and* NIGHTLIFE

> *un*official **TIP**
> Nightlife doesn't just mean stuff for the olds to do. There are plenty of kid-friendly activities after dark for the young ones. Check your resort's recreation schedule for campfires, movies on the beach or at the pool, and more.

WALT DISNEY WORLD and Universal Orlando are often thought of as vacations for kids that adults grudgingly go on and pay for. They can be that, but if you're willing to look, you'll find a few places that cater to adults after dark. First, check out your resort. Each Walt Disney World and Universal resort, from Fort Wilderness to Cabana Bay and the All-Star Resorts to the Hard Rock Hotel, has a watering hole for adults who need just a little something to take the edge off. Do we promise they'll be child-free? No, but go late, stay later, and enjoy some adult time. Even teetotalers can relax with a soda and take in the scene.

NIGHTLIFE AT WALT DISNEY WORLD RESORTS

DISNEY'S BOARDWALK OFFERS two adult-oriented venues, **Jellyrolls** and **Atlantic Dance Hall**. Jellyrolls is a dueling-piano bar that's open 7 p.m.–2 a.m. nightly (cover charge applies). Popular with locals, it's one of the few 21-and-up places you'll find at Walt Disney World. The entertainment is outstanding here. Across from Jellyrolls is **Atlantic Dance Hall**. It's often booked for private events, but on weekends it's open in the evenings (and has free admission). Atlantic Dance Hall has a DJ on hand and can be busy when large conventions are at the Swan and Dolphin or other Epcot-area resorts. Like Jellyrolls, Atlantic Dance Hall is 21-and-up.

At Coronado Springs, you'll find Disney's only true nightclub, **Rix Lounge**. This 5,000-square-foot upscale dance club and lounge is beautifully decorated, has a stellar tequila and margarita menu, features a DJ, and usually isn't busy unless there's a large convention on-site.

Other Walt Disney World resort bars with live entertainment are **Scat Cat's Lounge** at Port Orleans–French Quarter and **River Roost** at Port Orleans–Riverside. River Roost features **Ye Haa Bob Jackson,** an entertainer with a cult following among Disney fans. His fast-moving (and family-friendly) shows bring in locals and visitors from other resorts. Jackson's schedule is posted on his website, yehaabob.com. What he lacks in page-design skills, he more than makes up for with his skills at the piano and other instruments. Scat Cat's currently has karaoke and draws a crowd.

Trader Sam's Grog Grotto (inspired by the bar at the Disneyland Hotel in California) at the Polynesian Village is a delight. If you've ever found yourself in the *Enchanted Tiki Room* and thought to yourself, "You know, booze would really make this better," this is your place. For now, this lounge is extraordinarily busy, so be prepared to wait both to enter and to be served. While you're at it, pick up some souvenir tiki mugs for our collection (or start your own). See page 402 for a detailed review.

Our favorite nightspot at Walt Disney World, **Top of the World** at Bay Lake Tower, is for Disney Vacation Club members and their guests. If you're a member or you can hunt one down to take you up in return for a drink, try to stay after the Magic Kingdom fireworks when the bar clears out. The view and the setting are outstanding.

Cirque du Soleil *La Nouba* (closes December 31, 2017)

APPEAL BY AGE Under 21 ★★★★ 21–37 ★★★★★ 38–50 ★★★★ 51 and up ★★★★½

Type of show Circus as theater. Tickets and information ☎ 407-939-7600; cirque dusoleil.com/lanouba. Admission cost *Golden Circle:* $159.75 adults, $133.13 children ages 3–9; *Category Front & Center:* $145.91 adults, $120.34 children; *Category 1:* $129.93 adults, $106.50 children; *Category 2:* $101.17 adults, $83.07 children; *Category 3:* $82 adults, $67.09 children; *Category 4:* $67.09 adults, $55.38 children; all prices include tax. Cast size 72. Night of lowest attendance Thursday. Usual showtimes Tuesday–Saturday, 6 and 9 p.m. Authors' rating ★★★★★. Duration of presentation 1 hour, 45 minutes (no intermission) plus preshow.

DESCRIPTION AND COMMENTS *La Nouba* began its run at Disney Springs in 1998 and has been a great success by all accounts. These days, though, there

DISNEY DISH WITH JIM HILL

WHITHER CIRQUE DU SOLEIL? Cirque du Soleil's *La Nouba* closes New Year's Eve 2017 at Disney Springs after a 19-year run. What will replace it and anchor West Side? Disney will continue to partner with the circus from Quebec, possibly with a new show that pulls from Disney's vast collection of international programs. The theater will see a complete overhaul before any new show opens.

are many more traveling Cirque du Soleil shows than there were 19 years ago, which means people no longer need to go to Walt Disney World or Las Vegas or New York to experience it if they wish to.

La Nouba has seen updates, like replacing its high-wire and rope-jumping acts, but it remains the same high-energy, creative spectacle Cirque fans expect. It is at once a circus and more than a circus. The show combines a narrative with acrobatic acts and a moving musical score. *Unofficial Guide* readers consistently rate this as a highlight of their trip.

TOURING TIPS Be forewarned that the audience is an integral part of *La Nouba* and that at almost any time you might be plucked from your seat to participate. Our advice is to loosen up and roll with it. If you don't want to get involved, politely but firmly decline to be conscripted. Then fix a death grip on the arms of your chair. Tickets for reserved seats can be purchased in advance at the Cirque box office or over the phone using your credit card. Don't wait until the last minute; book well in advance from home, particularly as the show nears the end of its run at Disney Springs.

House of Blues

Type of show Live concerts with an emphasis on rock and blues. **Tickets and information** ☎ 407-934-BLUE (2583); hob.com. **Admission cost with taxes** From $11 for club nights to $25 and up depending on who's performing. **Nights of lowest attendance** Monday and Tuesday. **Usual showtimes** Vary between 7 p.m. and 9:30 p.m., depending on who's performing.

DESCRIPTION AND COMMENTS Developed by Blues Brother Dan Aykroyd, House of Blues comprises a restaurant and blues bar, as well as a concert hall. The restaurant serves Thursday–Saturday, 11:30 a.m.–11 p.m., and Friday–Saturday, 11:30 a.m.–1 a.m., which makes it one of the few late-night-dining options in Walt Disney World. Live music cranks up every night at 10:30 p.m. in the restaurant–blues bar, but even before then, the joint is way beyond 110 decibels. The music hall next door features concerts by an eclectic array of musicians and groups. During one visit, the show bill listed gospel, blues, funk, ska, dance, salsa, rap, zydeco, hard rock, groove rock, and reggae groups over a two-week period.

TOURING TIPS Prices vary from night to night according to the fame and drawing power of the featured band. Tickets ranged from $11 to $50 during our visits but go higher when a really big name is scheduled.

The music hall is set up like a nightclub, with tables and barstools for only about 150 people and standing room for a whopping 1,850. Folks dance when there's room and sometimes when there isn't. The tables and stools are first-come, first-served, with doors opening an hour before showtime on weekdays and 90 minutes before showtime on weekends. Acoustics are good, and the showroom is small enough to provide a relatively intimate concert experience. All shows are all ages unless otherwise indicated.

NIGHTLIFE AT UNIVERSAL ORLANDO RESORTS

WITH JUST FIVE (SOON TO BE SIX) on-site hotels, Universal Orlando doesn't have the variety in bars and lounges that you'll find at Disney, but what they do have is good. We love the **Swizzle** lobby bar at Cabana Bay, with its retro menu and great views of the resort's public spaces. **Jake's American Bar** at the Royal Pacific has great food and atmosphere. And **Velvet** at Hard Rock Hotel has super cocktails and unexpectedly good entertainment with its Velvet Sessions series (concert tickets cost extra).

LIVE MUSIC AT WALT DISNEY WORLD AND UNIVERSAL ORLANDO

YOU CAN FIND NATIONALLY KNOWN musical acts at **House of Blues** at Disney Springs West Side (see previous page) and **Hard Rock Cafe** in CityWalk.

Hard Rock Live at Hard Rock Cafe

Type of show Live rock/pop concerts with an emphasis on current and classic touring acts. **Tickets and information** ☎ 407-351-LIVE (5483); hardrock.com/live/locations/orlando. **Admission cost** Varies, depending on who's performing. **Usual showtimes** Vary between 7 p.m. and 9:30 p.m., depending on who's performing.

DESCRIPTION AND COMMENTS This 3,000-seat venue on the water at CityWalk draws nationally touring musicians and comics. There isn't a consistent theme to who plays here—we've seen everyone from Adam Ant to Wilco advertised, but Hard Rock definitely draws higher-profile performers than House of Blues. Of course, with great renown comes great admission prices—be prepared to pay as much to see an act at Hard Rock Live as you would at a large venue in any major city.

TOURING TIPS There is security at the doors here. Plan to arrive an hour before showtime.

Free Concerts at Disney World and Universal

EPCOT FESTIVAL OF THE ARTS Epcot's newest festival, which spans January and February (dates to be determined) includes concerts at the America Gardens Theatre. In 2017, the Disney on Broadway series was very popular, and we expect something similar to return for 2018.

GARDEN ROCKS Held during the Flower and Garden Festival, this series features classic rock acts, such as the members of Jefferson Starship who are still on speaking terms with each other.

SOUNDS LIKE SUMMER Tribute bands (such as ABBA impostors Bjorn Again and the Bon Jovi homage Slippery When Wet) play through most of June and July.

EAT TO THE BEAT Classic and current acts accompany your trip around the World Showcase during the Food and Wine Festival—if you count Wilson Phillips and Boyz II Men as current, that is.

Universal's Mardi Gras celebration features free concerts by a wide variety of acts, from up-and-comers to established groups and singers with songs on the charts to classic acts who bring in the nostalgia crowd. In the past, Universal has also presented a summer concert series, but that was temporarily suspended with the opening of Diagon Alley. It's still to be seen when and if the series will resume, but we believe it will.

PART SEVENTEEN

RECREATION, SPORTS, *and* SPAS

WALT DISNEY WORLD RECREATION

MOST WALT DISNEY WORLD GUESTS never make it beyond the theme parks, the water parks, or Disney Springs. Those who do, however, will discover an extraordinary selection of recreational opportunities, from guided fishing adventures and water-skiing outings to hayrides, horseback riding, fitness-center workouts, and minigolf. If you can do it at a resort, chances are good that it's available at Walt Disney World.

Boat, bike, and fishing-equipment rentals are handled on an hourly basis. Just show up at the rental office during operating hours and they'll fix you up. The same goes for the various fitness centers in the resort hotels. Golf, tennis, fishing expeditions, water-skiing excursions, hayrides, trail rides, and most spa services must be scheduled in advance. Though every resort features some selection of recreational options, those resorts on a navigable body of water generally offer the greatest variety. Also, the more upscale a resort, the more likely it is to have such amenities as a fitness center and spa.

RUN, DISNEY, RUN

WALT DISNEY WORLD STAGED its first long-distance road race—a 26.2-mile marathon—in January 1994. By hosting this one-day event, Disney hoped to attract a couple thousand people to Orlando during what would otherwise be the middle of a slow winter season. It was an immediate hit, drawing more than 7,000 runners and their families, most staying at a Disney hotel for longer than the one or two nights needed to run the race.

Disney added a Saturday half-marathon race to the event in 1998, just in time to catch the wave of popularity that distance running started enjoying around the turn of the millennium.

Today the **Walt Disney World Marathon Weekend** is a four-day affair, with a 5K on Thursday and a 10K on Friday. It's not uncommon to see 20,000 runners in the big races, and a few thousand hardy

BENEFITS TO RUNNING A DISNEY RACE

1. Every race runs through at least one theme park. The half-marathons go through Epcot and the Magic Kingdom, while the full marathon hits all four parks and most of the Magic Kingdom and Epcot resort areas. Even the smaller events are staged inside Epcot or Animal Kingdom.

2. The events are efficient and organized, with thousands of volunteers, top-notch entertainment all over the course, excellent first aid (we have experience), and great finisher medals.

3. Disney provides transportation between its hotels and the race venue, so your family can sleep in while you make your way to the start. Buses will also get you back to your hotel when you're finished.

4. Everyone qualifies. Unlike, say, the Boston Marathon, where you must run a marathon in under 4 hours before even thinking about getting in, the Disney races are open to everyone who can lace up some shoes.

5. The course is flat as a pancake. The steepest uphill is probably one of the on-ramps to Epcot on World Drive. If this is your first race, a flat course is one less thing to worry about. If you're a race veteran, this is a good opportunity to set a personal record.

souls run all four events (you get a special medal for doing so; it's appropriately of Dopey, one of Snow White's dwarfs).

Disney's race schedule has also expanded throughout the calendar and country, with no fewer than nine major races held in Disney World and Disneyland; see below for a complete schedule and summary of events. Disney even has a full-time staffed organization, **runDisney,** to coordinate and promote their events. Visit rundisney.com for the latest details. Prices are comparable to the big races in New York, Boston, and Chicago, but you don't get to run through Epcot in those.

unofficial **TIP**
It cost just over $2,500 in entry fees to run every Disney race in 2015. With airfare and hotels, expect to spend $12,000–$15,000.

As noted in Part One, *Unofficial Guide* staff and friends have run dozens of Disney races over the past decade, from simple 5Ks to the four-day, 48.6-mile 5K/10K/half-marathon/full-marathon combination (dubbed "The Dopey" for obvious reasons). If you've never run a distance race, Disney is the perfect first event for many reasons.

Here's a rundown of the major Disney races. For info on how they affect crowds, see "The Walt Disney World Calendar," page 50.

WALT DISNEY WORLD MARATHON WEEKEND (January 3–7, 2018) The largest Disney race of the year with more than 50,000 runners and their families. Races include a 5K, a 10K, and half and full marathons. The big variable is weather; we've run in freezing rain and we've run in 75°F sun. Check the forecast a couple of days before you leave.

DISNEY PRINCESS HALF-MARATHON WEEKEND (February 24–26, 2017) Races include a 5K, 10K, and half-marathon, which draw upwards of 25,000 runners. As its name implies, these events are designed for women, although around 2,000 men ran it in 2016. The weather is usually a bit warmer and more predictable than it is for January's race.

WINE & DINE HALF-MARATHON WEEKEND (November 2–5, 2017) Built around Epcot's fall Food & Wine Festival (see page 53), these races include a 5K and half-marathon. What makes the Wine & Dine half different is that it's held at night, with a typical start time around 10 p.m. Most years, the runners number about 13,000 or so. Although it's November, the weather can be quite warm, especially if you're used to training in cooler fall temperatures up north. The finish is in Epcot, where Disney provides entertainment and keeps open many of the Food & Wine kiosks.

Disney's newest race is the **Star Wars Half-Marathon—The Dark Side.** First held in April 2017, it includes Stormtroopers along the course, plus appearances by the other Star Wars characters, including Darth Vader. Because of construction at Disney's Hollywood Studios, expect the course to run through Epcot and the ESPN Wide World of Sports complex. A 5K and 10K race are offered in addition to the half.

Disneyland offers its own set of races, too. Runners who complete a race in both Disneyland and Disney World in the same year earn a special "coast to coast" medal. In addition, Disney has staged events from 5K to 10 miles themed to attractions such as Expedition Everest and the Tower of Terror. Those events aren't on the schedule at press time, but we wouldn't be surprised to see something like them in 2018.

Our blog has a number of articles on runDisney; search "runDisney" at blog.touringplans.com. Also check out the Mickey Miles podcast, run by our good friends Mike and Michelle, at mickeymilespodcast.com.

ESPN WIDE WORLD *of* SPORTS COMPLEX

THIS 220-ACRE, STATE-OF-THE-ART competition and training center consists of a 9,500-seat ballpark; a fieldhouse; and dedicated venues for baseball, softball, tennis, track and field, beach volleyball, and 27 other sports. From Little League Baseball to rugby, the complex hosts a mind-boggling calendar of professional and amateur competitions. It also hosts Disney's annual Night of Joy events (see page 52).

In late winter and early spring, the complex serves as the spring-training home of the Atlanta Braves. While Disney guests are welcome at the ESPN Wide World of Sports Complex as paying spectators (prices vary according to event), the facilities are unavailable to guests unless they're participants in a scheduled, organized competition. To learn which events, including Major League Baseball exhibition games, are scheduled during your visit, call ☎ 407-939-GAME (4263), or check the online calendar at espnwwos.com.

Admission is $18 for adults and $13 children for ages 3–9 (prices include tax). Some events carry an extra charge. There's a restaurant, the **ESPN Wide World of Sports Grill,** but no on-site lodging.

Off Osceola Parkway, on Victory Way, the complex has its own parking lot and is accessible via the Disney transportation system.

WALT DISNEY WORLD GOLF

DISNEY'S **Magnolia** and **Oak Trail Golf Courses,** across Floridian Way from the Polynesian Village Resort, envelop the recreational complex of the Shades of Green military resort, and the pro shops and support facilities adjoin the hotel proper. The **Magnolia** is a challenging, 18-hole course that used to be part of the PGA tour and underwent an extensive facelift in 2015; **Oak Trail** is a nine-hole, par-36 course for beginners.

The **Palm Golf Course,** in the same complex, underwent a major renovation by Arnold Palmer in 2013. Updates include modernized bunkers (94 of them!) and tees, and completely rebuilt greens. The Palm is 6,870 yards from the blue tees and 5,213 from the reds; it is designed for the midhandicap player.

unofficial **TIP**
Disney's golf courses are run by Arnold Palmer Golf Management. The late-2016 passing of Palmer has created renewed interest among travelers in his work.

It's business as usual for the **Lake Buena Vista Golf Course** at Saratoga Springs Resort & Spa, near Disney Springs.

All Disney golf courses are popular, with morning tee times at a premium, especially from January through April. Expect a round to take around 5 hours. Each location also has driving ranges and putting greens.

The peak season for all courses is January–May, and the off-season is May–October. Off-season and afternoon twilight rates are available. Carts, required at all courses except Oak Trail, are included in the greens fee. Tee times may be reserved 90 days in advance by Disney resort guests (including the Disney Springs Resort Area hotels and the Swan and Dolphin resorts) and 60 days in advance by day guests with a credit card. Proper golf attire, including spikeless shoes, is required. A collared shirt and Bermuda-length shorts or slacks meet the requirements.

In addition to the ability to book tee times farther in advance, guests of Walt Disney World–owned resorts get other benefits that may sway a golfer's lodging decision. These include discounted greens fees, club rental, and charge privileges. The single most important, and least known, benefit is the provision of free round-trip taxi transportation between the golf courses and your hotel, which lets you avoid moving your car or dragging your clubs on Disney buses. (Cabs are paid with vouchers supplied to hotel guests.)

unofficial **TIP**
To avoid the crowds, play on a Monday, Tuesday, or Wednesday, and sign up for a late-afternoon tee time.

The following chart summarizes prices for daily play at all Walt Disney World golf courses except Oak Trail; the cost of replaying the same course on the same day (if space is available) is half the full rate.

TYPE OF ADMISSION	OPENING–3 P.M.	3 –4 P.M.	4 P.M.–CLOSING
Resort guest	$126	$58	$58
Resort guest, 2-round pass	$150–$180	$150–$180	$150–$180
Day guest	$130	$58	$58
Day guest, 2-round pass	$175–$200	$175–$200	$175–$200

For more information, call ☎ 407-938-GOLF (4653), or book tee times at golfwdw.com.

Lake Buena Vista Golf Course ★★★

ESTABLISHED 1971 DESIGNER Joe Lee STATUS Resort

2200 Golf Dr., Lake Buena Vista, FL 32830; ☎ 407-938-GOLF (4653)

TEES
- **BLUE:** 6,745 yards, par 72, USGA 72.3, slope 133
- **WHITE:** 6,281 yards, par 72, USGA 70.1, slope 130
- **GOLD:** 5,910 yards, par 72, USGA 68.5, slope 125
- **RED:** 5,177 yards, par 72, USGA 69.7, slope 119

FACILITIES Pro shop, GPS-equipped carts, driving range, practice green, locker rooms, snack bar, food and beverage cart, club and shoe rentals.

COMMENTS There are several memorable holes here, but this layout is the only one at Disney with housing on it—a lot of housing—which detracts from the golfing experience. Nonetheless, Lake Buena Vista is relatively pristine as golf courses go—in fact, it has been certified by Audubon International as a Cooperative Wildlife Sanctuary. The setting is geographically unique among the other layouts; tucked behind Saratoga Springs, it has a swampy feel reminiscent of the area's pre-Disney wetlands, with trees dripping Spanish moss. The narrow fairways and small greens emphasize accuracy over length.

Magnolia Golf Course ★★★½

ESTABLISHED 1970 DESIGNER Joe Lee STATUS Resort

1950 W. Magnolia/Palm Dr., Lake Buena Vista, FL 32830; ☎ 407-938-GOLF (4653)

TEES
- **BLACK:** 7,516 yards, par 72, USGA 76.0, slope 141
- **BLUE:** 7,073 yards, par 72, USGA 74.0, slope 137
- **WHITE:** 6,558 yards, par 72, USGA 71.6, slope 130
- **GOLD:** 6,027 yards, par 72, USGA 69.0, slope 121
- **RED:** 5,127 yards, par 72, USGA 69.6, slope 126

FACILITIES Pro shop, GPS-equipped golf carts, driving range, practice green, locker rooms, food and beverage cart, club and shoe rentals.

COMMENTS Another Joe Lee creation, Magnolia is Disney's longest course and features a whopping 97 bunkers, including the famous one in the shape of Mickey Mouse's head. But the layout is slightly less challenging than the Palm's. Ten holes were lengthened and all greens resurfaced with TifEagle turf in 2005. This refurbishment added 300 yards to the already long course, and at more than 7,500 yards, it will be the longest most guests ever have the opportunity to play. Like the Palm, this course long hosted the PGA Tour (until 2012). In 2015, all 97 bunkers were rebuilt, along with improved cart paths and extensive tree work. Magnolia is certified by Audubon International as a Cooperative Wildlife Sanctuary.

Oak Trail Golf Course ★★½

ESTABLISHED 1980 DESIGNER Ron Garl STATUS Resort

1950 W. Magnolia/Palm Dr., Lake Buena Vista, FL 32830; ☎ 407-938-GOLF (4653)

TEES
- **WHITE:** 2,913 yards, par 36
- **RED:** 2,552 yards, par 36
- **JUNIOR:** 1,713 yards, par 36

FEES Adult $40; junior (ages 17 and under) $20. Pull carts $6 (course is walking only). Replaying the course costs an additional $19 for adults and $10 for junior players.

FACILITIES Pro shop, driving range, practice green, locker rooms, food and beverage cart, club and shoe rentals.

COMMENTS This Ron Garl nine-holer is a "real" course, not an executive par-3 like many nine-hole designs. Geared toward introducing children to the game, it also makes a good quick fix or warm-up before a round, and the walking-only layout is the only such routing at Disney. Oak Trail is certified by Audubon International as a Cooperative Wildlife Sanctuary.

Palm Golf Course ★★★★

ESTABLISHED 1970   DESIGNER Joe Lee   STATUS Resort

1950 W. Magnolia/Palm Dr., Lake Buena Vista, FL 32830; ☎ 407-938-GOLF (4653)

TEES
- **BLUE:** 6,870 yards, par 72, USGA 73.7, slope 131
- **WHITE:** 6,339 yards, par 72, USGA 71.4, slope 125
- **GOLD:** 5,995 yards, par 72, USGA 69.2, slope 118
- **RED:** 5,213 yards, USGA 70.5, slope 126

FACILITIES Pro shop, driving range, practice green, locker rooms, food and beverage cart, club and shoe rentals.

COMMENTS Completely renovated in 2013, with moderately difficult bunkers and undulating greens. The greens play medium-fast to fast, so either go with a lot of spin and loft or try to bounce your shot in. Carts have GPS screens. Staff service is excellent. Beware the alligator in the water at #9 (not kidding).

In Disney World (Sort Of)

Tranquilo Golf Club at Four Seasons Orlando ★★★★

ESTABLISHED 2014   DESIGNER Tom Fazio   STATUS Resort

151 Golf View Dr., Lake Buena Vista, FL 32830; ☎ 800-267-3046

TEES
- **TALON:** 7,039 yards, par 72, USGA 73.7, slope 127
- **CREST:** 6,629 yards, par 72, USGA 71.7, slope 124
- **WINGS:** 5,996 yards, par 72, USGA 68.8, slope 117
- **FEATHERS (W):** 5,283 yards, par 72, USGA 70.2, slope 124

FEES $135–$205 for 18 holes, including cart.

FACILITIES Pro shop, driving range, practice green, locker rooms, restaurant, club and shoe rentals.

COMMENTS Opened in 2014, Tranquilo Golf Club isn't technically a Disney course despite its location on Disney property, sitting on the former site of Disney's Osprey Ridge golf links. The course, which is also a certified Audubon wildlife sanctuary, is shared by Four Seasons Resort Orlando (see page 274) and Golden Oak, a Disney-owned luxury residential development. Tom Fazio, who designed the original course in 1992, also supervised this redesign. Updates include new contours for the greens, plus new and renovated bunkers. A par-3 hole (#16) features deep bunkering and sand, with a tiny green. Overall, Tranquilo is more challenging than the other Disney courses, which typically feature wide fairways and are forgiving, and is aimed more at the avid destination golfer. The course is open to the public.

Equally important at Tranquilo is the management by Four Seasons, which takes the same white-glove approach to its golf course portfolio as it does with its hotels. The course is impeccably maintained, with perhaps the best conditioning of any in the Orlando area, and has a stunning practice facility, clubhouse, and staff to match. Four Seasons also added a full-blown golf academy with both hourly and multiday instruction. Club carts use GPS technology to estimate your distance to the pin. The clubhouse's Plancha restaurant serves casual Cuban-American fare next to the lake.

MINIATURE GOLF

YEARS AGO, THE DISNEY INTELLIGENCE PATROL (DIP) noticed that as many as 113 guests a day were sneaking out of Disney World to play Goofy Golf. The thought of those truant guests making millionaires of minigolf entrepreneurs on I-Drive was enough to give a fat mouse ulcers. The response to this assault on Disney's market share was **Fantasia Gardens Miniature Golf,** an 11-acre complex with two 18-hole dink-and-putt golf courses. One is an "adventure" course, themed after Disney's animated film *Fantasia*. The other, geared more toward older children and adults, is an innovative approach-and-putt course with sand traps and water hazards.

Fantasia Gardens is beautifully landscaped and creatively executed. It features fountains, animated statues, topiaries, flower beds, and a multitude of other imponderables that you're unlikely to find at most minigolf courses.

Fantasia Gardens is located on Epcot Resorts Boulevard, across the street from the Swan Resort; it's open daily, 10 a.m.–11 p.m. To reach the course via Disney transportation, take a bus or boat to the Swan. The cost to putt, including tax, is $14 for adults and $12 for children ages 3–9. In case you arrive hungry or naked, Fantasia Gardens has a snack bar and a gift shop. For more information, call ☎ 407-WDW-PLAY (939-7529).

A Texas reader highly recommends the Disney minigolf courses:

Although we had a great time at every park and almost every meal, one of our best times was spent playing minigolf at Winter Summerland, outside Blizzard Beach. The theme of each course is wonderful and the golf challenging enough to be fun! Good times!

Winter Summerland is the other minigolf facility, next to Blizzard Beach water park. Winter Summerland offers two 18-hole courses: One has a "blizzard in Florida" theme, while the other sports a tropical-holiday theme. The Winter Summerland courses are much easier than the Fantasia Gardens courses, which makes them a better choice for families with preteen children. Operating hours and cost are the same as for Fantasia Gardens.

Our very favorite miniature-golf course in Orlando is **Hollywood Drive-In Golf,** in Universal CityWalk next to Universal Orlando's parking garage (just off the walkway to the parks; 6000 Universal Blvd.; ☎ 407-802-4848). One hole has the Creature from the Black Lagoon spitting water over the walkway that you have to pass through; another hole has a huge alien ship that you walk through and for which you need to press a button so that a door opens, Star Trek–style, to let you out. It's a nonstop barrage of clever in-jokes, insanely well-designed holes, and unique lighting elements. There's also a mobile app (for iOS and Android) for keeping score, plus misting fans for keeping cool. Open daily, 9 a.m.–2 a.m.; cost is $16 for adults, $14 for children ages 3–9. Two courses are available.

SERENITY NOW!
A Look at Disney-Area Spas

YOU'VE JUST SUGGESTED another theme park mini-marathon to your spouse, and from her barely audible murmur you realize she's debating which relative should get the kids when she stands trial for your homicide. Fortunately for you, Orlando is awash in spas ready to rub, wrap, and restore your loved one to domestic tranquility.

Note that the cost of a basic 1-hour massage is well over $100 before tip at most of these places. In an effort to get you the most inner peace for your money, we sent the *Unofficial Guide* research team to evaluate nine Walt Disney World–area spas.

At each resort, our team got a standard massage, a basic facial, and a manicure–pedicure combination. Each service was scheduled during a different week to ensure that one person's bad day didn't mar the whole evaluation. Also, we used the same researchers throughout the tests to ensure consistent comparisons of what is admittedly a somewhat subjective experience.

We rated each of the spas on the following pages on a scale of one star (poor) to five stars (excellent) in three areas: **Customer service** includes our interactions with the spa staff on everything from scheduling appointments to the actual treatments to follow-up questions after the visit. **Facilities** rates the amenities, functionality, and decor of the locker rooms, waiting areas, and equipment used before and after the services. **Amenities** rates the secondary spa offerings, such as food, pools, fitness centers, and the like. In addition, **sales pressure** (rated from low to high) indicates how hard the spa staff pushes you to buy products after your treatment. (Underlying our star system is a numerical quality scale of 0–100, so spas with the same overall star rating may have different numerical ratings.)

unofficial **TIP**
Check whether a gratuity has already been added to your bill before you pay. Most spas, including Disney's, tack on a tip of 18%–20%.

A fabulous money-saving idea is to find out if the spa you're interested in offers a day pass. These inexpensive tickets ($10–$55 among the spas we reviewed) typically allow use of the spa's fitness center, pool, sauna, steam room, and showers for an entire day.

Parents from Iowa City, Iowa, warn that spas have special rules for children:

> *When I called to schedule spa services, I was told that someone needed to be present with our 13-year-old girls for their massages. When we got there, we learned that someone had to be present with them at all times. This messed up the schedule that had been chosen for us by the spa reservation person and we all missed out on the whirlpool because we needed to sit with the girls for their mani–pedis. The girls ended up*

sitting with us for our mani-pedis for 2 hours with nothing else to do. The calling center was not well informed about the actual spa rules.

The Spa at Four Seasons Resort Orlando (see page 778) takes the No. 2 spot in our Orlando spa ratings. Like **Senses Spa at Disney's Grand Floridian Resort** (see page 777), the Four Seasons spa has all the bells and whistles (or, if you prefer, all the candles and soft lighting) you could hope for. Our reviewers tend to prefer the Grand Floridian's warmer decor just a tiny bit more than the Four Seasons' modern marble and tile. The reviewers also mention Senses' heated stone lounges and prewarmed robes as additional benefits. Service and amenities are excellent at any of the top spas in our chart, and you won't go wrong choosing any one of them.

ORLANDO SPAS RATED & RANKED

SPA	OVERALL RATING
1. SENSES SPA at Disney's Grand Floridian Resort	★★★★½
2. THE SPA at Four Seasons Resort Orlando	★★★★½
3. WALDORF ASTORIA SPA	★★★★
4. SENSES SPA at Disney's Saratoga Springs Resort	★★★★
5. (TIE) MANDARA SPA at Universal's Portofino Bay Hotel	★★★★
5. (TIE) RELÂCHE SPA at Gaylord Palms	★★★★
6. THE RITZ-CARLTON SPA, ORLANDO	★★★★
7. MANDARA SPA at the Dolphin	★★★½
8. THE SPA at Orlando World Center Marriott Resort	★★½

SPA PROFILES

Mandara Spa at Universal's Portofino Bay Hotel ★★★★

Universal Studios, 5601 Universal Blvd., Orlando; ☎ 407-503-1244; mandaraspa.com

Customer service ★★★★★. **Facilities** ★★★★½. **Amenities** ★★★. **Sales pressure** Medium. **Price range** $75–$275 spa services; $20–$155 hair and nail services; fitness pass, $10 hotel guests, $25 nonguests; 10%–20% discount for Universal Annual Pass holders; 10% discount for Florida residents Monday–Thursday; 20% service charge.

COMMENTS The Universal Orlando Mandara was renovated in 2013, retaining its Asian ambience despite its location in an Italy-themed resort. We like the contrast, though, and find it slightly exotic. Waiting areas are decorated in comforting earth tones; treatment rooms feature silk-draped ceilings. Changing and bathroom areas are spacious and clean, but they also include less-than-subtle advertisements for products sold on the premises. The remodeled treatment rooms feature additional decorative lighting and accessories.

The emphasis on tranquility extends to the stellar spa services, which included free self-heating oil for our massages. Men and women enjoy separate steam and sauna facilities; the whirlpool is unisex. The Portofino's sand-bottom pool is conveniently located near the entrance to the spa, as are nail services. The fitness center is still on the other side of the glass wall, however, so you may feel a bit like that doggy in the window.

Mandara Spa at the Dolphin ★★★½

Walt Disney World Dolphin, 1500 Epcot Resorts Blvd., Lake Buena Vista;
☎ 407-934-4772; mandaraspa.com

Customer service ★★★★★. Facilities ★★★. Amenities ★★★. Sales pressure High. **Price range** $70–$460 spa services; $20–$195 hair and nail services; 20% service charge.

COMMENTS Although the Mandaras at the Dolphin and the Portofino Bay Hotel share an Asian theme, everything is dialed down a notch at the Dolphin spa, starting with the waiting areas, of which there are two: the Meditation room, stocked with teas, water, and fruit, and the Consultation room, which is so close to the treatment rooms that voices occasionally disrupt the client's treatment experience.

Missing are the comfy sofas and chairs found at the Portofino Bay Mandara: At the Dolphin, it's standing room only. And we were surprised that both of this spa's two waiting rooms are unisex.

The treatment rooms, though pleasant, are also not on par with the Portofino Mandara's. Instead of silk-draped ceilings, an Asian-inspired wall hanging decorates one wall. Trappings aside, the Dolphin's spa also lacks a sauna, offering patrons only a coed steam room.

The one important asset that both Mandara spas have in common is exceptional treatments delivered by skilled staff. The Dolphin's employees seemed to be the most talkative of any we encountered.

Relâche Spa at Gaylord Palms ★★★★

Gaylord Palms Hotel & Convention Center, 6000 W. Osceola Parkway, Kissimmee;
☎ 407-586-4772; gaylordpalms.com/spa

Customer service ★★★★. Facilities ★★★★½. Amenities ★★★★. Sales pressure Low. **Price range** Price range $75–$410 spa services; $25–$100 nail services; 10% discount for Florida residents Monday–Friday; fitness pass, $30 hotel guests, $55 nonguests; 20% service charge.

COMMENTS *Relâche* means "relax" in French, and the name is no exaggeration. The staff's courtesy and professionalism were apparent from our initial phone call to our reception upon arrival to the technicians and assistants who worked on us. A complete tour of the facilities is given when you arrive, and you're encouraged to show up early to enjoy everything.

After changing into a comfy robe and slippers in a spacious and clean locker room, you're ushered into either the men's or women's waiting room, where lemon water, delicious teas, and fresh and dried fruits and nuts are provided. From there you move into the coed Tea Room, with more refreshments, very comfortable seating, and soft lights and music.

The soft lights and music continue in the immaculate treatment rooms. A facial includes neck, décolleté, hand, and foot massages. Luscious, fruity creams and serums are applied and are available for purchase afterward, but sales pressure is kept low.

Our manicure was just as enjoyable, with the same refreshments available. The nail salon is clean and comfortable. As with our facial, the products used during our treatments were waiting on a tray as we checked out, but there was no sales pressure.

The Ritz-Carlton Spa, Orlando ★★★★

4012 Central Florida Parkway, Orlando; ☎ 407-393-4200;
ritzcarlton.com/en/hotels/florida/orlando/spa

Customer service ★★★★★. Facilities ★★★★★. Amenities ★★★★★. Sales pressure Low–medium. Price range $145–$415 spa services; $50–$140 nail services; $50–$150 kids'/teens' services; 15% discount for Florida residents Monday–Thursday; 20% service charge.

COMMENTS The Ritz-Carlton Spa was so far ahead of anything else in Orlando when it opened almost a decade ago that it was in a class by itself. The facilities were much larger than anything in the area, and our interactions with the staff were the very definition of exemplary customer service. But while the service is still as fabulous as ever, the facilities are starting to look dated.

The spa is housed in a separate three-story building behind the main hotel. Every level is tastefully and elegantly decorated, including locker rooms, treatment rooms, and waiting rooms. Both single-sex and coed waiting areas are available. The waiting rooms and treatment rooms, while clean and functional, are showing their age, and our reviewer noted that they don't have niceties such as fresh flowers, mood lighting, or prewarmed robes—all of which the Senses spas at the Grand Floridian and Saratoga Springs offer.

Spa-goers also have the use of a separate whirlpool tub, sauna and steam rooms, and an outside lap pool where an attendant supplies complimentary towels, water, and sunscreen. All the equipment we used and observed was in working order during our visits.

Senses Spa at Disney's Grand Floridian Resort   ★★★★½

Grand Floridian Resort, 4401 N. Floridian Way, Lake Buena Vista;
☎ 407-939-7727; disneyworld.com/spas

Customer service ★★★★. Facilities ★★★★★. Amenities ★★★★. Sales pressure None. Price range $135–$495 spa services; $55–$95 nail services; $35–$50 kids' services (ages 4–12); 15%–20% off for Disney Annual Pass holders and Disney Vacation Club members; 20% service charge.

COMMENTS Reopened in 2013 after a much-needed total renovation, Senses at the Grand Floridian is modeled—and named—after the spas on the *Disney Dream* and *Disney Fantasy* cruise ships. The decor features cool greens and whites, with dark furniture and marble counters. Wallpaper in the lobby depicts an unspoiled Florida–as–Garden of Eden.

Treatment rooms have glass tile, marble countertops, and mosaic-tile walls. Facials include a paraffin treatment for your hands as well as a neck, shoulder, and décolleté massage. Our reviewer says, "The treatment bed was very comfortable, and the silky-feeling sheets are divine."

The Hand and Foot Spa was created by walling off part of the entrance lobby. Treatments here are sumptuous and include hand-arm and foot-leg massages. At the end of your treatment, you also receive a goodie bag that contains all the implements used, plus bottles of nail polish.

Massage beds are heated, and the treatments are likewise soothing and invigorating. You'll even get a prewarmed robe to relax in when you're done.

Sales pressure during our visits was nonexistent—no one asked us to buy anything, ever. The one downside to Senses is the waiting area: It gets a lot of foot traffic, so it's not as relaxing as it could be.

Senses Spa at Disney's Saratoga Springs Resort   ★★★★

1490-A Broadway, Lake Buena Vista; ☎ 407-939-7727; disneyworld.com/spas

Customer service ★★★★. Facilities ★★★★★. Amenities ★★★★. Sales pressure None. Price range $135–$495 spa services; $55–$95 nail services; $35–$50 kids' services (ages 4–12); 15%–20% off for Disney Annual Pass holders and Disney Vacation Club members; 20% service charge.

COMMENTS Saratoga Springs' spa was completely remodeled in 2013 to match the Senses Spa theming found on Disney's cruise ships and at its Grand Floridian Resort. Services, amenities, and prices at the Saratoga Springs Senses are in line with those at its Grand Floridian sibling, although the setting at Saratoga Springs is perhaps a little less formal. If you're staying at Saratoga Springs, Old Key West, or the Disney Springs Resort Area Hotels, or you're coming from an off-site hotel east of Disney World, we'd recommend the shorter drive and easier commute of the Senses at Saratoga Springs.

Our reviewer enjoyed the custom-made pedicure chairs at Saratoga Springs, as well as the heated massage tables. As with many spas' mani-pedi services, you'll get to keep a bottle of the nail polish you choose, for later touch-ups. It's a nice extra.

The Spa at Four Seasons Resort Orlando ★★★★½

10100 Dream Tree Blvd., Lake Buena Vista; ☎ 407 -313-7777; fourseasons.com/orlando/spa

Customer service ★★★★★. Facilities ★★★★½. Amenities ★★★★★. Sales pressure Low. Price range $160–$335 spa services; $25–$100 nail services; $35–$160 hair services.

COMMENTS If you've heard that you'll never have to open a door yourself at the Four Seasons, we're here to tell you it's true, at least at the Four Seasons' spa in Orlando. From parking the car (valet only, $5), to walking into the lobby, to the spa itself, we never touched a door.

The spa is located one level down from the lobby. After a quick orientation tour, we changed into luxurious robes (and less luxe rubber slippers) in our unisex locker room before heading to a coed waiting lounge with two fireplaces, which were roaring and welcome during our gloomy, damp fall visit. Snacks included various teas, a refreshing chilled fruit juice, blanched almonds, and dried and fresh fruit. One thing we'd like to see in the lounge is an ottoman so we could put our feet up while we wait.

Treatment rooms are new, clean, and attractive, with typical spa touches, including flowers, candles, soft lighting, and soft music. The massage was nice but seemed to end abruptly. After a break in the lounge, we were ready for our facial, which was wonderful; our aesthetician had a perfect touch. However, this treatment also ended abruptly; it almost seems as if the staff are on timers.

Brave spa-goers should try the Four Seasons' "Experience" showers—huge, nicely tiled, walk-in showers with a computer screen that lets you choose lighting, music, and different water pressures and spray patterns. There's no curtain or door, though, so wear a bathing suit if you desire.

The Spa at Orlando World Center Marriott Resort ★★½

8701 World Center Drive., Orlando; ☎ 407-238-8705; marriottworldcenter.com/spa

Customer service ★★★★. Facilities ★★. Amenities ★★★. Sales pressure High. Price range $100–$450 spa services; $40–$115 nail services; $10 fee to use steam room if you do not have a spa service scheduled.

COMMENTS In a small, separate building at the back of a sprawling hotel complex, The Spa at Orlando World Center Marriott Resort requires a hike from your room, or a really good set of directions if you're coming by car.

The women's locker room has no private changing areas; however, the bathroom stalls are big enough to make do. Spa-goers have the use of steam rooms and fitness facilities. Women should know that once they're in their spa robes, they're directed to a coed quiet room to await treatments. (On our visit, the spa was rife with male bonding.)

A staffer pressured us insistently to buy expensive oils and lotions after our treatments. Worse yet, the nail-drying equipment was either broken or nonexistent when we visited for our manicure: After shelling out $35 (plus tip), we were told to sit in the quiet room and blow on our nails to dry them.

Waldorf Astoria Spa ★★★★½

Waldorf Astoria Orlando, 14200 Bonnet Creek Resort Lane, Orlando;
☎ 407-597-5360; waldorfastoriaorlando.com/spa

Customer service ★★★★★. **Facilities** ★★★½. **Amenities** ★★★★★. **Sales pressure** None. **Price range** $160–$355 facials; $160–$460 massages; $45–$90 nail services; $65–$155 salon; day pass $20; 10% discount for Florida residents; complimentary valet parking (no self-parking); 20% service charge.

COMMENTS The Waldorf Astoria Spa is just a short walk from the lobby, and our first impression was very positive. Upon your arrival, an attendant takes you on a tour of the facilities. Once you are given your key, locker, robe, and slippers, you're free to wander the rooms before settling in the Tea Lounge. It's comfortable, but we like the lounge chairs at the Senses spas better.

The locker room and bathrooms are clean and modern. The showers are spacious and clean, with small iridescent tiles. Beyond these is the Tea Lounge, where your treatment person meets you—which is fortunate, because the place is big enough to get lost in.

Our massage, facial, and mani-pedi were all excellent. The pedicure came with Champagne. Clearly, these people know what we need.

APPENDIX

READERS' QUESTIONS *to the* AUTHORS

FOLLOWING ARE QUESTIONS AND COMMENTS from *Unofficial Guide* readers. Some frequently asked questions are addressed in every edition of the *Guide*.

QUESTION:

When you do your research, are you admitted to the parks for free? Do the Disney people know you're there?

ANSWER:

We pay regular admission; usually Disney doesn't know we're on-site. We pay for our own meals and lodging, both in and out of the World.

QUESTION:

How often is the Unofficial Guide *revised?*

ANSWER:

We publish a new edition once a year. The e-book (Kindle and ePub) is updated periodically after the print version is released.

QUESTION:

Where can I find information about what's changed at Walt Disney World in between published editions of the Unofficial Guide?

ANSWER:

We post important information online at **TouringPlans.com.**

QUESTION:

Do you write each new edition from scratch?

ANSWER:

Nope. When it comes to a destination the size of Walt Disney World, it's hard enough to keep up with what's new. Moreover, we put a lot of effort into communicating the most useful information in the clearest possible language. If an attraction or hotel has not changed, we're reluctant to tinker with its coverage for the sake of freshening the writing.

QUESTION:

I've never read any other Unofficial Guides. *Are they all as critical as* The Unofficial Guide to Walt Disney World?

ANSWER:

What some readers perceive as critical we see as objective and constructive. Our job is to prepare you for both the best and worst of Walt Disney World. As it happens, some folks are very passionate about what one reader calls "the inherent goodness of Disney." These readers might be more comfortable with press releases or the *Official Guide* than with the strong consumer viewpoint represented in our guide. That said, some readers take us to task for being overly *positive*.

QUESTION:

How many people have you surveyed for your age-group ratings regarding the attractions?

ANSWER:

Since the first *Unofficial Guide* was published in 1985, we've interviewed or surveyed almost 75,000 Walt Disney World patrons. Even with such a large survey population, however, we continue to find certain age groups underrepresented. Specifically, we'd love to hear more from seniors about their experiences with coasters and other thrill rides.

QUESTION:

Do you stay in Walt Disney World? If not, where?

ANSWER:

We stay at Walt Disney World lodging properties quite often. Since we began writing about Walt Disney World in 1982, we've stayed at all the Disney resorts and more than 100 different properties in various locations around Orlando, Lake Buena Vista, and Kissimmee.

QUESTION:

Bob, what's your favorite Florida attraction?

ANSWER:

What attracts me (as opposed to my favorite attraction) is **Juniper Springs,** a stunningly beautiful stream about 1½ hours north of Orlando in the Ocala National Forest. Originating in a limestone aquifer, the crystal-clear water erupts from the ground and begins a 10-mile journey to the creek's mouth at Lake George. Winding through palm, cypress, and live oak, the stream is more exotic than the Jungle Cruise, and alive with birds, turtles, and alligators. Put in at the Juniper Springs Recreation Area on FL 40, 36 miles east of Ocala. The 7-mile trip to the FL 19 bridge takes about 4½ hours. Canoe rentals and shuttle service are available at the recreation area. Call ☎ 352-625-3147 for more information.

READERS' COMMENTS

A WOMAN FROM SUWANEE, GEORGIA, offers a suggestion for the perfect Disney vacation:

> Your book made our trip a much more successful one. It also frustrated our male adults, who erroneously believed this was a trip for their enjoyment. We followed your advice to get up early and see as much as possible before an early lunch. But the men refused to go back to the hotel for a nap and a meal outside the park, so we fought the crowds until 3 or 4 p.m., by which time everyone was exhausted and cranky. My mother and I decided our next trip will include your guidebook and the children—but no men!

From a Greenville, Kentucky, mom who wasn't able to take advantage of the free-admission promotion on her daughter's birthday:

> We were disappointed that a birth certificate was the only acceptable ID for my daughter. We had certified shot records, and they still wouldn't accept them.

The weather is always, um, a hot topic with *Unofficial Guide* readers. First from a Poulsbo, Washington, reader:

> Holy hell, the Florida humidity is NO JOKE!

A Midwestern mom loved getting in the game, writing:

> It was a thrill for me to stand behind the ropes and wait until the park officially opened—to hear the music and announcements, then hurry with the throngs to the first ride. It was so exciting! My husband wasn't so thrilled. He teased me for days about running over old ladies and little children—I didn't run! I was speed-walking!

A woman from Mount Gretna, Pennsylvania, had some questions about theme park attire:

> I don't believe there was a section that addressed whether or not you could wear dresses on the rides. Quite a few amusement parks have security straps or bars that come up between one's knees, making it very difficult and immodest to wear dresses or skirts. Many women want to wear dresses for convenience, comfort, or cultural/religious convictions. I was concerned as I was packing whether this would limit any rides I could get on. I was quite pleased that it did not.

A Fenton, Missouri, woman evidently took her banker with her:

> Love your book! Our last trip was with eight people total: Grandma, Grandpa, my sister and her husband and two sons (ages 4 and 12), and my finance and me.

An Atlanta reader relates the story of a dirty bird and a solicitous cast member:

> While riding Splash Mountain, a mother and teenage son in our boat had brought ponchos (smart move), and the son took his off before we got out of the boat . . . just in time for a bird to poop on him. He went to buy a clean shirt in the gift shop, and when the cast member

found out what had happened, he gave the kid a free shirt. I thought that was very nice!

A Columbia, Missouri, woman offers advice for wives with anxious husbands:

A smartphone is the best thing in the world for keeping your husband busy in line. As long as mine had that phone, he could check e-mail, check dinner plans, and take and send pictures of the kids to family back home. He never complained about waiting in line, ever.

A Denver reader bursts our bubble (we thought we were Disney's favorites):

WDW cast members have an interesting reaction to the Guide. In one case, with the book in hand, we got an almost vampire-vs.-holy-water reaction from one CM (who then asked if he could take a quick peek).

There's just no pleasing some people—take this London bloke:

Why, oh why is Toy Story Mania! rated so highly? It's like playing crummy Wii games as someone pushes you around on your sofa.

From an exhausted mother:

Make sure moms are prepared for the fact that their kids will throw tantrums . . . and so will their husbands. Disney is a magical, wonderful thing, but it was also the most exhausting thing I have ever done. It required more patience than I've needed so far as a parent.

This Hawaii woman either is a record-holder of some sort or forgot to proofread before she hit SEND:

We've used the book for more than 90 years and love it. Keep up the good work!

From an opinionated Georgia family of four:

My 13-year-old son's one-word description of Space Mountain: "Awesome." My husband's one-word description: "Hell." My 10-year-old's best comment: "Hey Mom, here's a Disney motto that no one talks about: 'Bleed 'em dry.' " My 13-year-old's best comment as I was trying to get everyone to stop and pose in front of the topiaries: "Keep movin', Mom! There's no time for memories!"

A Somerville, Alabama, woman is succinct if nothing else:

Everything, other than my husband, was perfect.

From a woman who is more receptive after a couple of drinks:

We found (as an adult couple) that arriving early and leaving the parks for an afternoon drink or three in the monorail resorts was our saving grace! It also allowed my husband to convince me to go on more of the roller coasters!

And so it goes. . . .

ACCOMMODATIONS INDEX

See also the Restaurant Index on pages 789–792 and the Subject Index on pages 793–815.

See also the Restaurant Index on pages 789-792 and the Subject Index on pages 793-815.

See also the Restaurant Index on pages 789–792 and the Subject Index on pages 793–815.

See also the Restaurant Index on pages 789–792 and the Subject Index on pages 793–815.

RESTAURANT INDEX

Note: Page numbers of restaurant profiles are in **boldface** type.

See also the Accommodations Index on pages 784-788 and the Subject Index on pages 793-815.

See also the Accommodations Index on pages 784-788 and the Subject Index on pages 793-815.

See also the Accommodations Index on pages 784-788 and the Subject Index on pages 793-815.

SUBJECT INDEX

See also the Accommodations Index on pages 784–788 and the Restaurant Index on pages 789–792.

See also the Accommodations Index on pages 784–788 and the Restaurant Index on pages 789–792.

See also the Accommodations Index on pages 784–788 and the Restaurant Index on pages 789–792.

See also the Accommodations Index on pages 784–788 and the Restaurant Index on pages 789–792.

See also the Accommodations Index on pages 784–788 and the Restaurant Index on pages 789–792.

See also the Accommodations Index on pages 784–788 and the Restaurant Index on pages 789–792.

See also the Accommodations Index on pages 784–788 and the Restaurant Index on pages 789–792.

See also the Accommodations Index on pages 784–788 and the Restaurant Index on pages 789–792.

See also the Accommodations Index on pages 784–788 and the Restaurant Index on pages 789–792.

See also the Accommodations Index on pages 784–788 and the Restaurant Index on pages 789–792.

See also the Accommodations Index on pages 784-788 and the Restaurant Index on pages 789-792.

See also the Accommodations Index on pages 784–788 and the Restaurant Index on pages 789–792.

See also the Accommodations Index on pages 784–788 and the Restaurant Index on pages 789–792.

TOURING PLANS

"Not a Touring Plan"
TOURING PLANS

BELOW ARE THE SIMPLE RULES we use when friends ask us for touring plans that don't sound like a space shuttle launch checklist. Use these when you don't want the regimentation of a step-by-step plan but do want to avoid long waits in line. Skip attractions that don't suit you, and use FastPass+ if waits seem too long.

MAGIC KINGDOM

FOR ALL TOURING PLANS THAT BEGIN AT PARK OPENING On days when the Magic Kingdom does not host morning Extra Magic Hours, arrive 50–70 minutes before official opening. On days when the Magic Kingdom has morning EMH, arrive 40 minutes ahead. As soon as you enter the park, get in line for the walk to Seven Dwarfs Mine Train.

FOR PARENTS OF SMALL CHILDREN WITH ONE DAY TO TOUR, ARRIVING AT PARK OPENING *Note:* Use FastPass+ wherever you can get it. See Fantasyland first, starting with Seven Dwarfs Mine Train and Peter Pan's Flight. See Frontierland and some of Adventureland, and then take a midday break. Return to the park and complete your tour of Adventureland. Next, meet characters at the Town Square Theater and tour Tomorrowland. End on Main Street for fireworks.

FOR ADULTS WITH ONE DAY TO TOUR, ARRIVING AT PARK OPENING *Note:* Use FastPass+ for attractions in the late morning and midafternoon, especially in Frontierland and Tomorrowland. See Seven Dwarfs Mine Train and Peter Pan's Flight in Fantasyland, and then head to Liberty Square. Tour Frontierland, Adventureland, and Tomorrowland next. End on Main Street for fireworks.

FOR PARENTS AND ADULTS WITH TWO DAYS TO TOUR *Note:* Day one works great for Disney resort guests on Extra Magic Hours mornings. Use FastPass+ where you can. Start day one with Seven Dwarfs Mine Train in Fantasyland; then tour Liberty Square and Frontierland before leaving the park around midday. Begin day two in Tomorrowland; then tour Adventureland. End on Main Street for fireworks.

FOR PARENTS AND ADULTS WITH AN AFTERNOON AND A FULL DAY *Note:* The full day works great for Disney resort guests on Extra Magic Hours mornings. For the afternoon, tour Frontierland, Adventureland, and Tomorrowland (get FastPass+ reservations for Splash and Space Mountains and Big Thunder Mountain Railroad). On your full day of touring, see Fantasyland, Liberty Square, and Tomorrowland again (for any missed attractions from the previous afternoon). End on Main Street for fireworks.

EPCOT

FOR PARENTS AND ADULTS WITH ONE DAY TO TOUR, ARRIVING AT PARK OPENING Ride Soarin' and Test Track (use the single-rider line if possible), and then Mission: Space (Orange) (FastPass+ suggested start time: 9:30 a.m.). Eat lunch and ride Spaceship Earth (FastPass+ suggested start time: 1 p.m.). Then tour World Showcase counterclockwise, starting in Canada (FastPass+ suggested start time for Frozen Ever After: 7 p.m.). End the day with *IllumiNations*.

FOR PARENTS AND ADULTS WITH ONE DAY TO TOUR, ARRIVING LATE MORNING Tour Future World West except for Soarin'. Then tour World Showcase counterclockwise, starting in Canada (FastPass+ suggested start time for Frozen Ever After: 3 p.m.). Tour Future World East, including Test Track (use the single-rider line if possible); then ride Spaceship Earth (FastPass+ suggested start time: 5 p.m.). Now ride Soarin' and tour the remainder of Future World West. End the day with *IllumiNations*.

FOR PARENTS AND ADULTS WITH TWO DAYS TO TOUR On day one, start with Test Track and Mission: Space (Orange) (FastPass+ suggested start times: 9:30 a.m.). See the rest of Future World as you desire, and then tour Mexico through the United States in World Showcase (FastPass+ suggested start time for Frozen Ever After: 2 p.m.). On day two, ride Soarin' in The Land (FastPass+ suggested start time: 9 a.m.), and then tour Canada through Japan in World Showcase. End your day with *IllumiNations* (use FastPass+).

DISNEY'S ANIMAL KINGDOM

FOR PARENTS AND ADULTS ARRIVING AT PARK OPENING Get FastPass+ reservations for Avatar Flight of Passage in Pandora, plus Expedition Everest in Asia and Kilimanjaro Safaris; then begin a land-by-land, counterclockwise tour of the park, starting in Pandora. Work in shows as you near them, but leave *Finding Nemo—The Musical* for last. Eat dinner and end the night with *The Awakening* and *Rivers of Light*.

FOR PARENTS AND ADULTS ARRIVING LATE MORNING Get FastPass+ reservations for Avatar Flight of Passage in Pandora and Kilimanjaro Safaris in Africa; then begin a counterclockwise tour of the park, starting in Africa and saving Kali River Rapids and Expedition Everest for last. Eat dinner and end the night with *The Awakening* and *Rivers of Light*.

DISNEY'S HOLLYWOOD STUDIOS

IF TOY STORY LAND IS NOT OPEN:

FOR ADULTS ARRIVING AT PARK OPENING Obtain FastPass+ reservations for Toy Story Mania! (FastPass+ suggested start time: 10 a.m.). Then begin a counterclockwise tour of the park with Rock 'n' Roller Coaster, Tower of Terror, and The Great Movie Ride. Work in shows as you near them. End the tour with *Voyage of the Little Mermaid*. End the day on Sunset Boulevard for *Fantasmic!* (If you're staying for the show, FastPass+ for Tower of Terror in the last hour the park is open would work well.)

FOR PARENTS AND ADULTS ARRIVING LATE MORNING Get FastPass+ reservations for Toy Story Mania! and use those at the appropriate time; otherwise, save it for last. Start a clockwise tour of the park with Muppet-Vision 3-D, and end with Toy Story Mania! if you didn't use FastPass+. Then grab a bite to eat, and see *Fantasmic!*

IF TOY STORY LAND IS OPEN:

FOR ADULTS ARRIVING AT PARK OPENING Obtain late-morning FastPass+ reservations for Slinky Dog Dash or Toy Story Mania! Then begin a counterclockwise tour of the park with Rock 'n' Roller Coaster, Tower of Terror, and The Great Movie Ride. Visit Toy Story Land next. Work in shows as you near them. End the day on Sunset Boulevard for *Fantasmic!* (If you're staying for the show, FastPass+ for Tower of Terror in the last hour the park is open would work well.)

FOR PARENTS AND ADULTS ARRIVING LATE MORNING Get FastPass+ reservations for Slinky Dog Dash or Toy Story Mania! and use those at the appropriate time; otherwise, save it for last. Start a clockwise tour of the park with Star Tours and end with Toy Story Land. Then grab a bite to eat, and see *Fantasmic!*

The Magic Kingdom

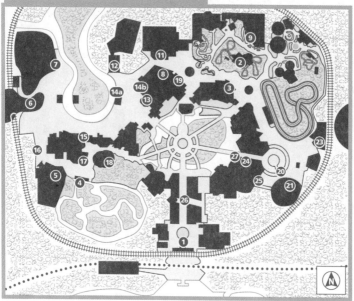

MAGIC KINGDOM ONE–DAY TOURING PLAN FOR ADULTS

1. Arrive at the Magic Kingdom entrance 40 minutes (when Morning Extra Magic Hours are in effect) to 70 minutes (on days without Morning EMHs) before official opening. Get guide maps and the *Times Guide*.

2. As soon as Main Street opens, head toward Fantasyland and get in line for the Seven Dwarfs Mine Train. Ride as soon as the park opens.

3. Ride The Many Adventures of Winnie the Pooh.

4. Head to Adventureland and take Jungle Cruise.

5. Ride Pirates of the Caribbean.

6. In Frontierland, ride Splash Mountain.

7. Ride Big Thunder Mountain Railroad.

8. In Fantasyland, ride Peter Pan's Flight.

9. Ride Under the Sea: Journey of the Little Mermaid.

10. Eat lunch.

11. Ride It's a Small World in Fantasyland.

12. In Liberty Square, see The Haunted Mansion.

13. Work in a viewing of *The Muppets Present . . . Great Moments in American History* around the next step.

14. See *The Hall of Presidents* and ride the *Liberty Belle* Riverboat.

15. In Frontierland, see *Country Bear Jamboree*.

16. In Adventureland, play a game of A Pirate's Adventure: Treasures of the Seven Seas.

17. See *Walt Disney's Enchanted Tiki Room*.

18. Explore the Swiss Family Treehouse.

19. In Fantasyland, see *Mickey's PhilharMagic*.

20. In Tomorrowland, ride the Tomorrowland Transit Authority PeopleMover.

21. See *Walt Disney's Carousel of Progress*.

22. Eat dinner.

23. In Tomorrowland, ride Space Mountain.

24. See *Monsters, Inc. Laugh Floor* in Tomorrowland.

25. Ride Buzz Lightyear's Space Ranger Spin.

26. If an evening parade is scheduled, see it from Main Street, U.S.A.

27. See the evening castle light show and fireworks. A good viewing spot is on the bridge between the Central Plaza and Tomorrowland.

Suggested FastPass+ reservations and start times: Seven Dwarfs Mine Train, 9 a.m.; Big Thunder Mountain Railroad, 10 a.m.; Peter Pan's Flight, 11 a.m. **Suggested day-of FastPass+ reservations:** After using your 11 a.m. Peter Pan FastPass+, make a FastPass+ reservation for The Haunted Mansion for around 1 p.m. After you've experienced Haunted Mansion, make a FastPass+ reservation for Space Mountain around 7 p.m.

If any of these FastPasses or times aren't available, see tinyurl.com/free-tplans to customize the plan based on the FastPasses you *were* able to get, at no charge. You can also get free real-time updates while you're in the park.

The Magic Kingdom

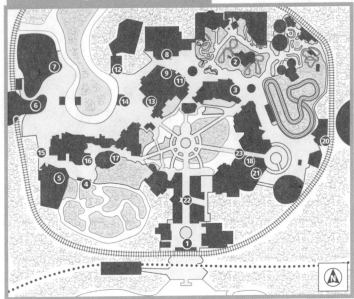

MAGIC KINGDOM AUTHORS' SELECTIVE
ONE-DAY TOURING PLAN FOR ADULTS

1. Arrive at the Magic Kingdom entrance 40 minutes (when Morning Extra Magic Hours are in effect) to 70 minutes (on days without Morning EMHs) before official opening. Get guide maps and the *Times Guide*.

2. As soon as the park opens, head to Fantasyland and get in line to ride the Seven Dwarfs Mine Train.

3. Ride The Many Adventures of Winnie the Pooh.

4. Head to Adventureland and take Jungle Cruise.

5. Ride Pirates of the Caribbean.

6. In Frontierland, ride Splash Mountain.

7. Ride Big Thunder Mountain Railroad.

8. Ride It's a Small World in Fantasyland.

9. Experience Peter Pan's Flight.

10. Eat lunch.

11. In Fantasyland, see *Mickey's PhilharMagic*.

12. In Liberty Square, see The Haunted Mansion.

13. Experience *The Hall of Presidents* or see a showing of *The Muppets Present . . . Great Moments in American History*.

14. Ride the *Liberty Belle* Riverboat.

15. In Adventureland, play a game of A Pirate's Adventure: Treasures of the Seven Seas.

16. See *Walt Disney's Enchanted Tiki Room*.

17. Explore the Swiss Family Treehouse.

18. See *Monsters, Inc. Laugh Floor* in Tomorrowland and enjoy some free time before dinner.

19. Eat dinner.

20. In Tomorrowland, ride Space Mountain.

21. Ride Buzz Lightyear's Space Ranger Spin and enjoy some free time before the fireworks.

22. If an evening parade is scheduled, see it from Main Street, U.S.A.

23. See the evening castle light show and fireworks. A good viewing spot is on the bridge between the Central Plaza and Tomorrowland.

Suggested FastPass+ reservations and start times: Seven Dwarfs Mine Train, 9 a.m.; Big Thunder Mountain Railroad, 10 a.m.; Peter Pan's Flight, 11 a.m. **Suggested day-of FastPass+ reservations:** After using your 11 a.m. Peter Pan FastPass+, make a FastPass+ reservation for The Haunted Mansion for around 1 p.m. After you've experienced Haunted Mansion, make a FastPass+ reservation for Space Mountain around 7 p.m.

If any of these FastPasses or times aren't available, see tinyurl.com/free-tplans to customize the plan based on the FastPasses you *were* able to get, at no charge. You can also get free real-time updates while you're in the park.

The Magic Kingdom

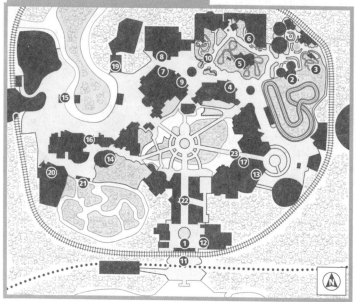

MAGIC KINGDOM ONE-DAY TOURING PLAN
FOR PARENTS WITH SMALL CHILDREN
(Review the Small-Child Fright-Potential Chart on pages 432–435.)

1. Arrive at the Magic Kingdom entrance 40 minutes (when Morning Extra Magic Hours are in effect) to 70 minutes (on days without Morning EMHs) before official opening. Rent strollers before the park opens. Get guide maps and the *Times Guide*.

2. As soon as the park opens, head to Fantasyland's Storybook Circus area and ride Dumbo the Flying Elephant.

3. Ride The Barnstormer.

4. Ride The Many Adventures of Winnie the Pooh.

5. Take the Seven Dwarfs Mine Train.

6. Ride Under the Sea: Journey of the Little Mermaid.

7. Experience Peter Pan's Flight.

8. Take the It's a Small World boat ride.

9. See *Mickey's PhilharMagic*.

10. See *Enchanted Tales with Belle*.

11. Eat lunch and take a midday break.

12. Return to the park and meet Mickey Mouse at Town Square Theater.

13. Experience Buzz Lightyear's Space Ranger Spin.

14. In Adventureland, tour the Swiss Family Treehouse.

15. In Frontierland, take the raft over to Tom Sawyer Island. Allow at least 30 minutes to explore the island, Fort Langhorn, and the barrel bridges.

16. See *Country Bear Jamboree*.

17. In Tomorrowland, see the *Monsters, Inc. Laugh Floor* either before or after dinner.

18. Eat dinner.

19. In Liberty Square, ride The Haunted Mansion.

20. In Adventureland, ride Pirates of the Caribbean.

21. Take the Jungle Cruise.

22. If an evening parade is scheduled, see it from Main Street, U.S.A.

23. See the evening castle light show and fireworks. A good viewing spot is on the bridge between the Central Plaza and Tomorrowland.

Suggested FastPass+ reservations and start times: Seven Dwarfs Mine Train, 9 a.m.; Peter Pan's Flight, 10 a.m.; *Enchanted Tales with Belle*, 11 a.m. **Suggested day-of FastPass+ reservations:** After using your 11 a.m. *Enchanted Tales* FastPass+, make a FastPass+ reservation for Buzz Lightyear's Space Ranger Spin for around 4 p.m. After you've experienced Buzz, make a FastPass+ reservation for The Haunted Mansion around 6 p.m.

  If any of these FastPasses or times aren't available, see tinyurl.com/free-tplans to customize the plan based on the FastPasses you *were* able to get, at no charge. You can also get free real-time updates while you're in the park.

The Magic Kingdom

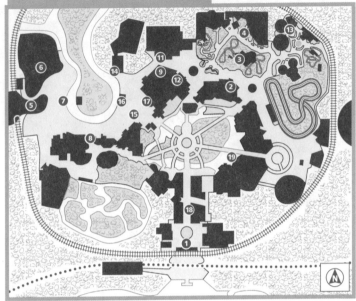

MAGIC KINGDOM TWO-DAY TOURING PLAN FOR ADULTS: DAY ONE

1. Arrive at the Magic Kingdom entrance 40 minutes (when Morning Extra Magic Hours are in effect) to 70 minutes (on days without Morning EMHs) before official opening. Rent strollers before the park opens if needed. Get guide maps and the *Times Guide*.

2. As soon as the park opens, head to Fantasyland and get in line to ride The Many Adventures of Winnie the Pooh.

3. Take the Seven Dwarfs Mine Train.

4. Ride Under the Sea: Journey of the Little Mermaid.

5. In Frontierland, ride Splash Mountain.

6. Experience Big Thunder Mountain Railroad.

7. Take the raft over to Tom Sawyer Island. Allow at least 30 minutes to explore the island, Fort Langhorn, and the barrel bridges.

8. Return to Frontierland and see *Country Bear Jamboree*.

9. See Peter Pan's Flight in Fantasyland.

10. Eat lunch.

11. Ride It's a Small World in Fantasyland.

12. See *Mickey's PhilharMagic*.

13. Meet a couple of Disney characters at Pete's Silly Sideshow in Storybook Circus.

14. In Liberty Square, ride The Haunted Mansion.

15. Catch a showing of *The Muppets Present . . . Great Moments in American History* around the next two steps. You may have a few hours of free time between steps 17 and 18.

16. Take a ride on the *Liberty Belle* Riverboat.

17. See *The Hall of Presidents*.

18. If an evening parade is scheduled, see it from Main Street, U.S.A.

19. See the evening castle light show and fireworks. A good viewing spot is on the bridge between the central hub and Tomorrowland.

Suggested FastPass+ reservations and start times: Seven Dwarfs Mine Train, 9 a.m.; Big Thunder Mountain Railroad, 10 a.m.; Peter Pan's Flight, 11 a.m.

If any of these FastPasses or times aren't available, see tinyurl.com/free-tplans to customize the plan based on the FastPasses you *were* able to get, at no charge. You can also get free real-time updates while you're in the park.

The Magic Kingdom

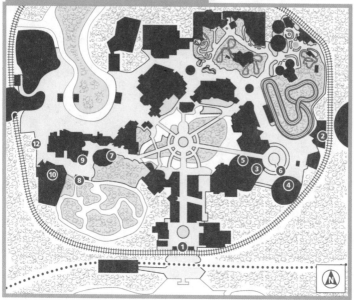

MAGIC KINGDOM TWO-DAY TOURING PLAN FOR ADULTS: DAY TWO

1. Arrive at the Magic Kingdom entrance 50 minutes (Disney resort guests) to 70 minutes (non-Disney resort guests) before opening. Get guide maps and the *Times Guide.*

2. As soon as the park opens, head to Tomorrowland and ride Space Mountain.

3. Experience Buzz Lightyear's Space Ranger Spin.

4. See *Walt Disney's Carousel of Progress.*

5. See the *Monsters, Inc. Laugh Floor.*

6. Ride the Tomorrowland Transit Authority PeopleMover.

7. In Adventureland, tour the Swiss Family Treehouse.

8. Take the Jungle Cruise.

9. Experience *Walt Disney's Enchanted Tiki Room.*

10. Ride Pirates of the Caribbean.

11. Eat lunch.

12. Play a game of A Pirates Adventure: Treasure of the Seven Seas.

13. Tour the rest of the park and meet characters who interest you. Check the daily entertainment schedule for showtimes.

Suggested FastPass+ reservations and start times: Space Mountain, 9 a.m.; Jungle Cruise, 10 a.m.; Pirates of the Caribbean, 11 a.m.

If any of these FastPasses or times aren't available, see tinyurl.com/free-tplans to customize the plan based on the FastPasses you *were* able to get, at no charge. You can also get free real-time updates while you're in the park.

The Magic Kingdom

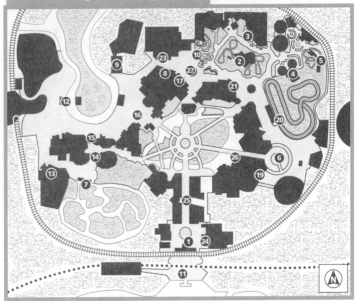

MAGIC KINGDOM DUMBO-OR-DIE-IN-A-DAY TOURING PLAN
FOR PARENTS WITH SMALL CHILDREN
(Review the Small-Child Fright-Potential Chart on pages 432–435.
Interrupt the plan for meals, rest, and a cocktail or two.)

1. Arrive at the Magic Kingdom entrance 50 minutes (Disney resort guests) to 70 minutes (non–Disney resort guests) before opening. Rent strollers before the park opens. Get maps and *Times Guide*.
2. As soon as Main Street, U.S.A., opens, get in line for the walk to Seven Dwarfs Mine Train. Ride when park opens.
3. Ride Under the Sea: Journey of the Little Mermaid.
4. Ride Dumbo the Flying Elephant. Ride again. (*Tip:* Stand in line about 48 people behind the other parent and child. When the first parent is done riding, hand the child to the second parent in line.)
5. Ride The Barnstormer.
6. In Tomorrowland, ride the Astro Orbiter.
7. Take the Jungle Cruise in Adventureland.
8. Return to Fantasyland to ride Peter Pan's Flight.
9. In Liberty Square, see The Haunted Mansion.
10. See *Enchanted Tales with Belle*.
11. Eat lunch and take a midday break of at least 3 hours outside the park.
12. In Frontierland, take the raft over to Tom Sawyer Island. Allow at least 30 minutes to explore the island, Fort Langhorn, and the barrel bridges.
13. In Adventureland, ride Pirates of the Caribbean.
14. Ride The Magic Carpets of Aladdin.
15. In Frontierland, see *Country Bear Jamboree*.
16. In Liberty Square, catch a showing of *The Muppets Present . . . Great Moments in American History.*
17. In Fantasyland, see *Mickey's PhilharMagic*.
18. Eat dinner.
19. Ride Buzz Lightyear's Space Ranger Spin in Tomorrowland.
20. Take a spin on the Tomorrowland Speedway.
21. Back in Fantasyland, ride The Many Adventures of Winnie the Pooh.
22. Ride the Prince Charming Regal Carrousel.
23. Ride It's a Small World.
24. Meet Mickey Mouse at Town Square Theater on Main Street, U.S.A.
25. If an evening parade is scheduled, see it from Main Street.
26. See the evening castle light show and fireworks. A good viewing spot is on the bridge between the Central Plaza and Tomorrowland.

Suggested FastPass+ reservations and start times: Seven Dwarfs Mine Train, 9 a.m.; Peter Pan's Flight, 10 a.m.; *Enchanted Tales with Belle*, 11 a.m. **Suggested day-of FastPass+ reservations:** Make a Pirates of the Caribbean FastPass+ reservation for around 3:30 p.m. Make a Haunted Mansion reservation for around 6 p.m. After you've used your last FastPass+, check for FastPass+ reservations for *Happily Ever After* fireworks.

If any of these FastPasses or times aren't available, see tinyurl.com/free-tplans to customize the plan based on the FastPasses you *were* able to get, at no charge. You can also get free real-time updates while you're in the park.

Epcot

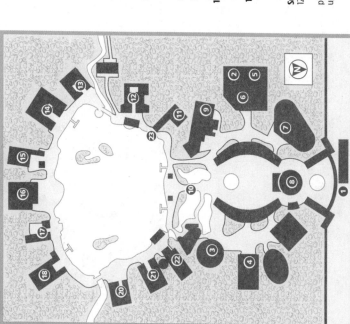

EPCOT ONE-DAY TOURING PLAN FOR ADULTS

1. Arrive 40 minutes before opening. Get guide maps and the *Times Guide*.

2. As soon as the park opens, ride Soarin' in The Land.

3. Ride Test Track in Future World East. Take advantage of the single-rider line if you can.

4. Ride Mission: Space (Orange).

5. Take the Living with the Land boat ride at The Land.

6. Eat lunch. Sunshine Seasons at The Land is a good choice.

7. See The Seas with Nemo & Friends.

8. Ride Spaceship Earth.

9. Experience Journey Into Imagination with Figment.

10. Play a game of Agent P's World Showcase Adventure. Sign up for a mission on the main walkway from Future World to World Showcase.

11. Begin a counterclockwise tour of World Showcase with the Canada Pavilion and *O Canada!* film.

12. Tour the United Kingdom Pavilion.

13. Visit France and see *Impressions de France.*

14. Tour Morocco.

15. Explore Japan.

16. See *The American Adventure.*

17. Visit Italy.

18. Tour Germany.

19. Eat dinner.

20. Explore China and see *Reflections of China.*

21. Tour the Norway Pavilion and take the Frozen Ever After boat ride. Stop in at the stave church on the way out of Norway.

22. Tour Mexico and ride the Gran Fiesta Tour.

23. See *IllumiNations.* Prime viewing spots are along the lagoon between Canada and France. You could also try for a late dinner; get a lagoon-side table at La Cantina or La Hacienda de San Angel in Mexico (Advance Reservations needed at the latter), or try Spice Road Table in Morocco.

Suggested FastPass+ reservations and start times: Mission: Space (Orange), 10:15 a.m.; Spaceship Earth, 12:30 p.m.; Frozen Ever After, 7:30 p.m.

If any of these FastPasses or times aren't available, see tinyurl.com/free-tplans to customize the plan based on the FastPasses you *were* able to get, at no charge. You can also get free real-time updates while you're in the park.

EPCOT AUTHORS' SELECTIVE ONE-DAY TOURING PLAN FOR ADULTS

1. Arrive 40 minutes before opening. Get guide maps and the *Times Guide*.

2. As soon as the park opens, ride Soarin' in The Land.

3. Ride Test Track in Future World East.

4. Ride Mission: Space (Orange).

5. Take the Living with the Land boat ride at The Land.

6. Eat lunch. Sunshine Seasons at The Land is a good choice.

7. Ride Spaceship Earth.

8. See The Seas with Nemo & Friends in Future World West.

9. Play a game of Agent P's World Showcase Adventure. Sign up for a mission on the main walkway from Future World to World Showcase.

10. Begin a counterclockwise tour of World Showcase with the Canada Pavilion and *O Canada!* film.

11. Tour the United Kingdom Pavilion.

12. Visit France and see *Impressions de France*.

13. Tour Morocco.

14. Explore Japan.

15. See *The American Adventure*.

16. Visit Italy.

17. Tour Germany.

18. Eat dinner.

19. Explore China and see *Reflections of China*.

20. Tour the Norway Pavilion. Try the Frozen Ever After boat ride if the wait is 25 minutes or less. Stop in at the stave church on the way out of Norway.

21. Tour Mexico and ride the Gran Fiesta Tour.

22. See *IllumiNations*. Prime viewing spots are along the lagoon between Canada and France. You could also try for a late dinner; get a lagoon-side table at La Cantina or La Hacienda de San Angel in Mexico (Advance Reservations needed at the latter), or try Spice Road Table in Morocco.

Suggested FastPass+ reservations and start times: Test Track, 9:15 a.m.; Mission: Space (Orange), 10:15 a.m.; Spaceship Earth, 12:30 p.m.

If any of these FastPasses or times aren't available, see tinyurl.com/free-tplans to customize the plan based on the FastPasses you *were* able to get, at no charge. You can also get free real-time updates while you're in the park.

Epcot

Epcot

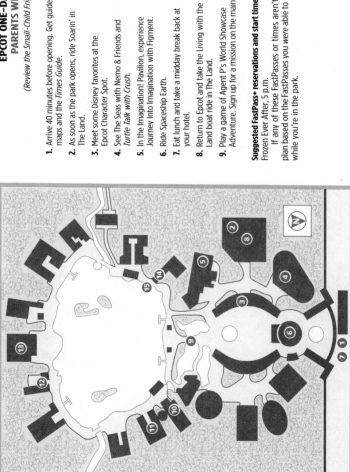

EPCOT ONE-DAY TOURING PLAN FOR PARENTS WITH SMALL CHILDREN

(Review the Small-Child Fright-Potential Chart on pages 432–435.)

1. Arrive 40 minutes before opening. Get guide maps and the *Times Guide*.

2. As soon as the park opens, ride Soarin' in The Land.

3. Meet some Disney favorites at the Epcot Character Spot.

4. See The Seas with Nemo & Friends and *Turtle Talk with Crush*.

5. In the Imagination! Pavilion, experience Journey Into Imagination with Figment.

6. Ride Spaceship Earth.

7. Eat lunch and take a midday break back at your hotel.

8. Return to Epcot and take the Living with the Land boat ride in The Land.

9. Play a game of Agent P's World Showcase Adventure. Sign up for a mission on the main walkway from Future World to World Showcase.

10. Begin a clockwise tour of World Showcase with the Mexico Pavilion. Take the Gran Fiesta Tour boat ride.

11. Tour Norway. Take the Frozen Ever After boat ride. If your children are interested, meet Anna and Elsa at the Royal Sommerhus.

12. Tour the Italy Pavilion.

13. See *The American Adventure*.

14. Tour Canada and see the *O Canada!* film.

15. See *IllumiNations*. Prime viewing spots are along the lagoon between Canada and France. You could also try for a late dinner; get a lagoon-side table at La Cantina or La Hacienda de San Angel in Mexico (Advance Reservations needed at the latter), or try Spice Road Table in Morocco.

Suggested FastPass+ reservations and start times: Epcot Character Spot, 9:15 a.m.; Spaceship Earth, 11 a.m.; Frozen Ever After, 5 p.m.

If any of these FastPasses or times aren't available, see tinyurl.com/free-tplans to customize the plan based on the FastPasses you *were* able to get, at no charge. You can also get free real-time updates while you're in the park.

Epcot

EPCOT TWO-DAY EARLY-RISER TOURING PLAN: DAY ONE

*(Parents with young children should review the
Small-Child Fright-Potential Chart on pages 432–435.)*

1. Arrive 40 minutes before opening. Get guide maps and the *Times Guide.*

2. As soon as the park opens, ride Soarin' at The Land in Future World West.

3. Ride Test Track in Future World East. This 0.6-mile round-trip will allow you to skip the standby line at Frozen Ever After on day two.

4. Return to Future World West and ride Living with the Land in The Land.

5. In the Imagination! Pavilion, experience Journey Into Imagination with Figment.

6. Eat lunch.

7. See The Seas with Nemo & Friends and *Turtle Talk with Crush.*

8. If you're interested in playing Agent P's World Showcase Adventure, sign up for a mission on the main walkway from Future World to World Showcase.

9. Tour Canada and see the *O Canada!* film.

10. Visit the United Kingdom Pavilion.

11. Tour France and see *Impressions de France.*

12. Explore Morocco, including the art museum up front.

13. Visit Japan.

Suggested FastPass+ reservations and start times: Test Track, 9:30 a.m.; Journey Into Imagination with Figment, 10:30 a.m.; The Seas with Nemo & Friends, 12:30 p.m.

If any of these FastPasses or times aren't available, see tinyurl.com/free-tplans to customize the plan based on the FastPasses you *were* able to get, at no charge. You can also get free real-time updates while you're in the park.

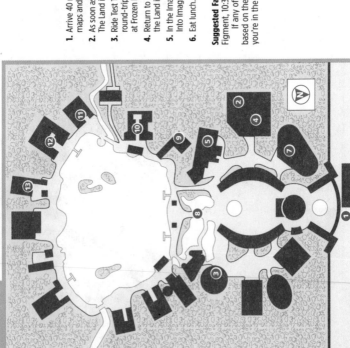

EPCOT TWO-DAY EARLY-RISER TOURING PLAN: DAY TWO

(Parents with young children should review the Small-Child Fright-Potential Chart on pages 452–435.)

1. Arrive 40 minutes before opening. Get guide maps and the *Times Guide.*

2. Ride Mission: Space (Orange).

3. Experience *Ellen's Energy Adventure.*

4. See Colortopia in Innoventions East.

5. Ride Spaceship Earth.

6. Eat lunch.

7. If you're interested in playing Agent P's World Showcase Adventure, sign up for a mission on the main walkway from Future World to World Showcase.

8. Begin a clockwise tour of the east side of World Showcase at Mexico. Take the Gran Fiesta Tour boat ride.

9. Explore Norway and take the Frozen Ever After boat ride.

10. Tour China and see *Reflections of China.*

11. Visit Germany.

12. See Italy.

13. See *The American Adventure.*

14. See *IllumiNations.* Prime viewing spots are along the lagoon between Canada and France. You could also try for a late dinner; get a lagoon-side table at La Cantina or La Hacienda de San Angel in Mexico (Advance Reservations needed at the latter), or try Spice Road Table in Morocco.

Suggested FastPass+ reservations and start times: Mission: Space (Orange), 9:30 a.m.; Spaceship Earth, 11 a.m.; Frozen Ever After, 1:30 p.m.

If any of these FastPasses or times aren't available, see tinyurl.com/free-tplans to customize the plan based on the FastPasses you *were* able to get, at no charge. You can also get free real-time updates while you're in the park.

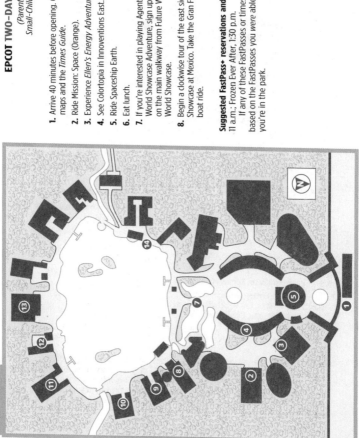

Epcot

Disney's Animal Kingdom

DISNEY'S ANIMAL KINGDOM ONE-DAY TOURING PLAN
(Assumes: Avatar Flight of Passage, Na'Vi River Journey, Expedition Everest, and Kilimanjaro Safaris are in the same "choose only 1" FastPass+ tier.)

1. Arrive 40 minutes prior to official opening. Get guide maps and the *Times Guide*.

2. As soon as the park opens, take the Na'Vi River Journey in Pandora.

3. Ride Avatar Flight of Passage.

4. In Asia, ride Expedition Everest.

5. In DinoLand U.S.A., ride Dinosaur.

6. Take a spin on Primeval Whirl.

7. In Asia, experience the Maharaja Jungle Trek.

8. Eat lunch.

9. In Africa, experience the Kilimanjaro Safaris.

10. Take the Wildlife Express Train from Africa to Rafiki's Planet Watch. Tour Conservation Station and the rest of the area. Take the train back to Africa.

11. Walk the Gorilla Falls Exploration Trail.

12. See *Festival of the Lion King*.

13. Play a few rounds of Wilderness Explorers around the next three steps.

14. See *Flights of Wonder* in Asia.

15. Walk the Discovery Island Trails to observe the nature exhibits.

16. See *Finding Nemo—The Musical* in DinoLand U.S.A.

17. Eat dinner.

18. Ride the Kali River Rapids in Asia.

19. See *The Awakening* at The Tree of Life from Discovery Island.

20. Tour Pandora after dark, if time permits.

21. See *Rivers of Light*. If two shows are performed, the second one is usually less crowded.

Suggested FastPass+ reservations and start times: Flight of Passage: 9–10 a.m. Expedition Everest: 10–11 a.m. Kilimanjaro Safaris: 12:30–1:30 p.m. **Suggested day-of FastPass+ reservations:** Kali River Rapids, starting around 8 p.m. An alternative FastPass+ option would be for *Rivers of Light*, if available.

If any of these FastPasses or times aren't available, see tinyurl.com/free-tplans to customize the plan based on the FastPasses you *were* able to get, at no charge. You can also get free real-time updates while you're in the park.

Disney's Hollywood Studios

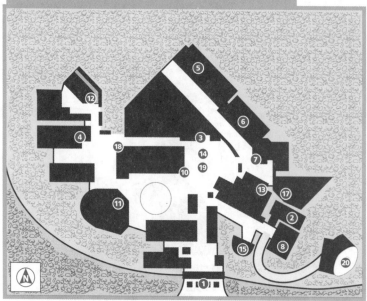

DISNEY'S HOLLYWOOD STUDIOS ONE-DAY TOURING PLAN
(Toy Story Land not yet open)

1. Arrive at the park 30–40 minutes before official opening time. Get guide maps and the *Times Guide*.

2. As soon as the park opens, ride Rock 'n' Roller Coaster at the end of Sunset Boulevard.

3. Ride The Great Movie Ride.

4. In Echo Lake, experience Star Tours—The Adventures Continue.

5. Ride Toy Story Mania! in Pixar Place.

6. See *Walt Disney: One Man's Dream*.

7. See *Voyage of the Little Mermaid* in Animation Courtyard.

8. Ride The Twilight Zone Tower of Terror at the end of Sunset Boulevard.

9. Eat lunch.

10. See the *For the First Time in Forever: A Frozen Sing-Along Celebration.*

11. See *Indiana Jones Epic Stunt Spectacular!* in Echo Lake.

12. See *Muppet-Vision 3-D* in Muppet Courtyard.

13. In Animation Courtyard, work in *Disney Junior— Live on Stage!* if you have small children.

14. See the *Star Wars: A Galaxy Far, Far Away* stage show on Hollywood Boulevard.

15. See *Beauty and the Beast—Live on Stage*.

16. Eat dinner.

17. Tour Star Wars Launch Bay in Animation Courtyard.

18. Meet Minnie and Mickey in Red Carpet Dreams.

19. See the evening fireworks if they're being presented.

20. Enjoy *Fantasmic!* Plan on arriving about an hour early to get good seats. If there are two shows, the second is less crowded.

Suggested FastPass+ reservations and start times: Star Tours—The Adventures Continue, 9 a.m.; Toy Story Mania!, 10 a.m.; The Twilight Zone Tower of Terror, 11 a.m. **Suggested day-of FastPass+ reservation:** *Fantasmic!*, after you ride Tower of Terror.

If any of these FastPasses or times aren't available, see tinyurl.com/free-tplans to customize the plan based on the FastPasses you *were* able to get, at no charge. You can also get free real-time updates while you're in the park.

Disney's Hollywood Studios

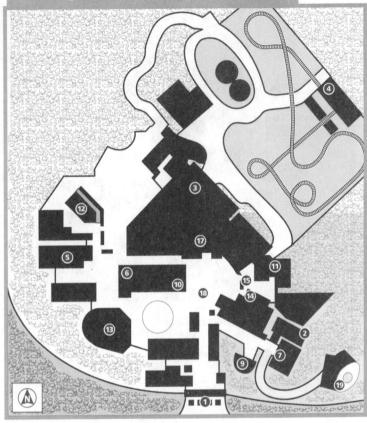

DISNEY'S HOLLYWOOD STUDIOS ONE-DAY TOURING PLAN
(with Toy Story Land open)
(Assumes Slinky Dog Dash will be in the same FastPass+ tier as Toy Story Mania! and Rock 'n' Roller Coaster)

1. Arrive at the park 30–40 minutes before official opening time. Get guide maps and the *Times Guide.*
2. As soon as the park opens, ride Rock 'n' Roller Coaster at the end of Sunset Boulevard.
3. Ride Toy Story Mania! in Toy Story Land.
4. Do the Slinky Dog Dash.
5. In Echo Lake, ride Star Tours— The Adventures Continue.
6. Meet Mickey and Minnie Mouse at Red Carpet Dreams.
7. Ride the Tower of Terror on Sunset Boulevard.
8. Eat lunch around the next two shows.
9. See *Beauty and the Beast—Live on Stage.*
10. See *For the First Time in Forever: A Frozen Sing-Along Celebration.*
11. Tour the Star Wars Launch Bay in Animation Courtyard.
12. Experience *Muppet-Vision 3-D* in Muppet Courtyard.
13. See the *Indiana Jones Epic Stunt Spectacular!* in Echo Lake.
14. If you have small children, see *Disney Junior— Live on Stage!*
15. Catch a performance of *Star Wars: A Galaxy Far, Far Away* if time permits.
16. Eat dinner.
17. Ride The Great Movie Ride.
18. See the evening fireworks—currently *Star Wars: A Galactic Spectacular.*
19. See *Fantasmic!*

Suggested FastPass+ reservations and start times: Star Tours—The Adventures Continue, 9 a.m.; Toy Story Mania!, 10 a.m.; The Twilight Zone Tower of Terror, 11 a.m. **Suggested day-of FastPass+ reservation:** *Fantasmic!*, after you ride Tower of Terror.

If any of these FastPasses or times aren't available, see tinyurl.com/free-tplans to customize the plan based on the FastPasses you *were* able to get, at no charge. You can also get free real-time updates while you're in the park.

Universal's Islands of Adventure

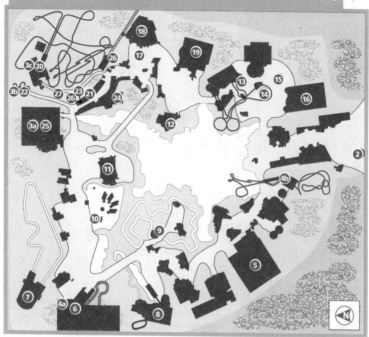

UNIVERSAL'S ISLANDS OF ADVENTURE ONE-DAY TOURING PLAN FOR ADULTS

1. Buy admission in advance. Call ☎ 407-363-8000 the day before for the official opening time.

2. Arrive at IOA 75–90 minutes before the official opening time if Early Park Admission is offered and you're eligible, or 30–45 minutes before opening for day guests. Get a park map as soon as you enter.

3. Early-entry guests should ride Harry Potter and the Forbidden Journey (**3a**). Ride Flight of the Hippogriff (**3b**) and Dragon Challenge (**3c**) as well, if you have time.

4. Early-entry guests can exit Hogsmeade into Jurassic Park as early entry ends and ride Skull Island: Reign of Kong (**4a**) as soon as it opens, then continue to Marvel Super Hero Island to ride The Incredible Hulk Coaster (**4b**). Guests without early entry should start at this step with the Hulk.

5. Ride The Amazing Adventures of Spider-Man.

6. Experience Skull Island: Reign of Kong (if you haven't already).

7. Take the Jurassic Park River Adventure. Put your belongings in a pay locker here and leave them through the next two water rides.

8. Reverse course to ride Dudley Do-Right's Ripsaw Falls in Toon Lagoon.

9. Ride Popeye & Bluto's Bilge-Rat Barges. Retrieve your property from Jurassic Park.

10. Explore Camp Jurassic.

11. If time permits before lunch, check out the exhibits in the Jurassic Park Discovery Center.

12. Eat lunch. A good sit-down choice is Mythos (make reservations at opentable.com).

13. Ride The High in the Sky Seuss Trolley Train Ride! in Seuss Landing.

14. Ride the Caro-Seuss-el.

15. Ride One Fish, Two Fish, Red Fish, Blue Fish.

16. Ride The Cat in the Hat.

17. In Lost Continent, chat with the Mystic Fountain.

18. See the next scheduled performance of *The Eighth Voyage of Sindbad*.

19. Experience *Poseidon's Fury*.

20. If you haven't already done so, enter The Wizarding World of Harry Potter–Hogsmeade, and ride Dragon Challenge, or walk through the queue to see the Triwizard Tournament artifacts.

21. See the *Frog Choir* or *Triwizard Spirit Rally* perform on the small stage outside Hogwarts, time permitting.

22. Ride Flight of the Hippogriff if you didn't do so back in Step 3b.

23. See the wand ceremony at Ollivanders and buy a wand if you wish.

24. Have dinner at Three Broomsticks.

25. See the stage show in Step 21 if you haven't already done so. Pose for a picture with the Hogwarts Express conductor, and explore Hogsmeade's shops and interactive windows.

26. Ride Harry Potter and the Forbidden Journey. If the wait is more than 30 minutes, request a castle tour to experience the queue, and then use the single-rider line.

27. Remain in Hogsmeade until closing, enjoying the atmosphere, or revisit any favorite attractions.

Universal Studios Florida

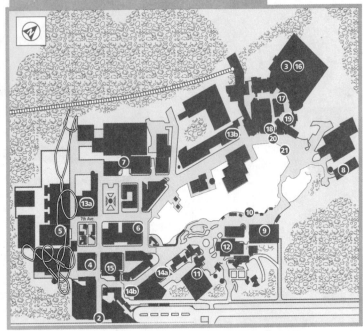

UNIVERSAL STUDIOS FLORIDA ONE-DAY TOURING PLAN FOR ADULTS
(Assumes: Day guest without Universal Express; 1-Day Base Ticket)

1. Buy your admission in advance and call ☎ 407-363-8000 the day before your visit for the official opening time.

2. Arrive at USF 90–120 minutes before the official opening time if Early Park Admission is offered and you're eligible, or 30–45 minutes before opening for day guests. Get a park map and use Universal's smartphone app to reserve Virtual Line times for Jimmy Fallon and/or Fast & Furious (opens 2018) for early afternoon.

3. Early-entry guests should ride Harry Potter and the Escape from Gringotts if it's operating. If not, enjoy the rest of Diagon Alley but don't get in line.

4. Before early entry ends, hotel guests should exit Diagon Alley and ride Despicable Me Minion Mayhem. Day guests should wait in the front lot until permitted to ride Despicable Me.

5. Ride Hollywood Rip Ride Rockit.

6. Experience Transformers: The Ride 3-D.

7. Ride Revenge of the Mummy in New York.

8. Ride Men in Black Alien Attack in World Expo.

9. Experience The Simpsons Ride.

10. Ride Kang & Kodos' Twirl 'n' Hurl if 50 or fewer people are in line.

11. Ride E.T. Adventure in Woody Woodpecker's KidZone.

12. Work in *Animal Actors on Location!* around lunch (we recommend Fast Food Boulevard), according to the daily entertainment schedule.

13. Experience Race Through New York Starring Jimmy Fallon (**13a**) and/or Fast & Furious:

Supercharged (**13b**), according to the Virtual Line reservations you made earlier.

14. See *Universal Orlando's Horror Make-Up Show* (**14a**) and *Terminator 2: 3-D* (**14b**) according to the daily entertainment schedule.

15. See *Shrek 4-D* in Production Central.

16. By this time, you should be able to enter Diagon Alley without waiting, even on busy days. Ride Harry Potter and the Escape from Gringotts. If this is your first ride, take the standby queue. For rerides, use the single-rider line. The Gringotts queue may close before the rest of the park if the posted wait time exceeds remaining operating hours by more than 60 minutes.

17. See the *Celestina Warbeck* and *Tales of Beedle the Bard* shows.

18. See the wand ceremony at Ollivanders and buy a wand if you wish.

19. Tour Diagon Alley. Browse the shops, explore the dark recesses of Knockturn Alley, and discover the interactive effects. If you're hungry, try the Leaky Cauldron or Florean Fortescue's Ice-Cream Parlour.

20. Chat with the Knight Bus conductor and his shrunken head. Also look for Kreacher in the window of 12 Grimmauld Place, and listen to the receiver in the red phone booth.

21. If scheduled, see *Universal's Cinematic Spectacular* from Central Park (directly across the lagoon from Richter's), Duff Brewery, or the embankment in front of London.

Universal Studios Florida

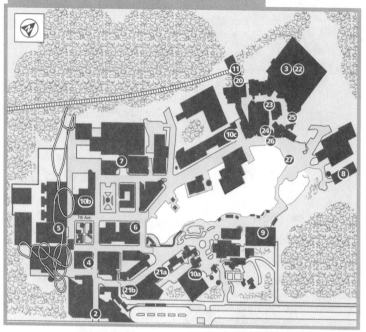

THE BEST OF UNIVERSAL STUDIOS FLORIDA AND ISLANDS OF ADVENTURE IN ONE DAY

(Assumes: 1-Day Park-to-Park Ticket)

1. Buy your admission in advance; call ☎ 407-363-8000 the day before your visit for the official opening time.

2. Arrive at USF 90–120 minutes before the official opening time if Early Park Admission is offered and you're eligible, or 30–45 minutes before opening for day guests. Line up at the shortest open turnstile, and get a park map and use Universal's smartphone app to reserve Virtual Line times for Jimmy Fallon and/or Fast & Furious (opens 2018) for midmorning or late afternoon.
   Alternative: If only IOA is open for Early Park Admission and you're eligible, arrive at IOA's turnstiles 75–90 minutes before the official opening time. Ride Harry Potter and the Forbidden Journey (**2a**). Ride Flight of the Hippogriff (**2b**) and Dragon Challenge (**2c**) if you have time. Take Hogwarts Express (**2d**) to King's Cross Station before USF officially opens for the day, and continue at the next step.

3. Early-entry guests should ride Harry Potter and the Escape from Gringotts if it is operating. If not, enjoy the rest of Diagon Alley but don't get in line.

4. Before early entry ends, hotel guests should exit Diagon Alley and ride Despicable Me Minion Mayhem. Day guests should wait in the front lot until permitted to ride Despicable Me.

5. Ride Hollywood Rip Ride Rockit.

6. Experience Transformers: The Ride 3-D in Production Central.

7. Ride Revenge of the Mummy in New York.

8. Ride Men in Black Alien Attack in World Expo.

9. Experience The Simpsons Ride.

10. If you have small children, ride E.T. Adventure (**10a**) in Woody Woodpecker's KidZone. If not, experience Race Through New York Starring Jimmy Fallon (**10b**) or Fast & Furious: Supercharged (**10c**) (opens 2018) according to the Virtual Line reservations you made earlier. If you couldn't get a return line, check at the attractions an hour or two before closing.

11. Ride Hogwarts Express from King's Cross Station to IOA. Have your park-to-park ticket ready.

12. Ride Dragon Challenge in The Wizarding World of Harry Potter–Hogsmeade.

13. Eat lunch at Mythos in Lost Continent (**13a**) or Three Broomsticks in Hogsmeade (**13b**).

14. Ride The Incredible Hulk Coaster on Marvel Super Hero Island.

15. Ride The Amazing Adventures of Spider-Man.

16. Continue clockwise through Toon Lagoon, and ride the Reign of Kong on Skull Island.

(Continued on next page)

Universal's Islands of Adventure

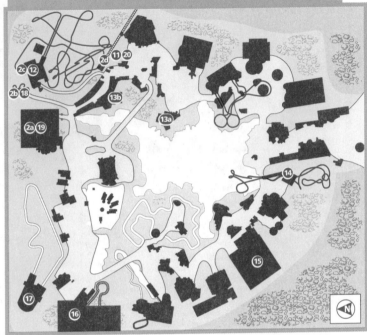

THE BEST OF UNIVERSAL STUDIOS FLORIDA AND ISLANDS OF ADVENTURE IN ONE DAY

(Continued from previous page)

17. Experience Jurassic Park River Adventure.

18. Enter Hogsmeade, and ride Flight of the Hippogriff if the wait isn't too long.

19. Ride Harry Potter and the Forbidden Journey. If the wait is more than 30 minutes, request a castle tour to experience the queue, and then use the single-rider line.

20. Return to Universal Studios Florida using the Hogwarts Express from Hogsmeade Station, or walk back to the other park if the posted wait exceeds 20 minutes.

See map on previous page for the following steps.

21. See the next showing of *Universal Orlando's Horror Make-Up Show* (21a) upon returning to USF. If the remaining *Horror Make-Up* showtimes aren't convenient, substitute with *Terminator 2: 3-D* (21b). Also remember your return time for any remaining Virtual Line reservations you made. If you couldn't get a return line, check at the attractions an hour or two before closing

22. By this time, you should be able to enter Diagon Alley without waiting, even on busy days. Ride Harry Potter and the Escape from Gringotts. If

this is your first ride, take the standby queue. For rerides, use the single-rider line. The Gringotts queue may close before the rest of the park if the posted wait time exceeds remaining operating hours by more than 60 minutes.

23. See the *Celestina Warbeck* and *Tales of Beedle the Bard* shows.

24. See the wand ceremony at Ollivanders and buy a wand if you wish.

25. Tour Diagon Alley. Browse the shops, explore the dark recesses of Knockturn Alley, and discover the interactive effects. If you're hungry, try the Leaky Cauldron or Florean Fortescue's Ice-Cream Parlour.

26. Chat with the Knight Bus conductor and his shrunken head. Also look for Kreacher in the window of 12 Grimmauld Place, and listen to the receiver in the red phone booth.

27. If scheduled, watch *Universal's Cinematic Spectacular* from Central Park (directly across the lagoon from Richter's), Duff Brewery, or the embankment in front of London.

Typhoon Lagoon

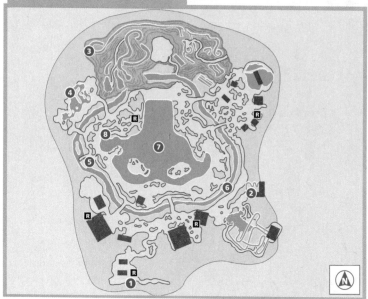

TYPHOON LAGOON ONE-DAY TOURING PLAN
FOR PARENTS WITH SMALL CHILDREN

1. Arrive at the park entrance 30 minutes before opening. Take care of locker and towel rentals at Singapore Sal's, to your right after you've walked along the winding entrance path and emerged into the park. Find a spot to stow the remainder of your gear, noting any nearby landmarks to help you find your way back.

2. Ride Miss Adventure Falls as many times as you like.

3. Ride Gangplank Falls as many times as you like.

4. If your kids enjoyed Gangplank Falls, try Keelhaul Falls if it seems appropriate.

5. Enjoy the Ketchakiddee Creek kids' play area.

6. Grab some tubes and ride Castaway Creek. A complete circuit takes 20–25 minutes.

7. Swim in the Surf Pool as long as you like.

8. Ride the Bay Slides in the Surf Pool.

9. Repeat your favorite attractions as desired.

Blizzard Beach

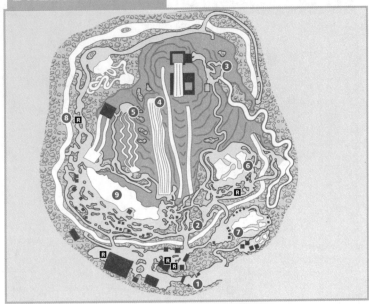

BLIZZARD BEACH ONE-DAY TOURING PLAN
FOR PARENTS WITH SMALL CHILDREN

1. Arrive at the park entrance 30 minutes before opening. Take care of locker and towel rentals at Lottawatta Lodge, to your left as you enter the park. Find a spot to stow the remainder of your gear, noting any nearby landmarks to help you find your way back.

2. Take the chairlift up Mount Gushmore to the Green Slope. *Note:* It might be faster—but more tiring—to walk to the top.

3. Raft down Teamboat Springs. Repeat as much as you like while the park is still uncrowded.

4. If your kids are up for it, try the Toboggan Racers.

5. If the kids enjoyed the Toboggan Racers, try the Snow Stormers next.

6. Visit the Ski Patrol Training Camp.

7. Visit Tike's Peak.

8. Grab some tubes and ride Cross Country Creek.

9. Swim in Melt-Away Bay's Wave Pool for as long as you like.

MAGIC KINGDOM **TOURING PLAN COMPANION**

ATTRACTION | RECOMMENDED VISITATION TIMES | AUTHORS' RATING

Ariel's Grotto *(FastPass+)* | Before 10:30 a.m., in the 2 hours before closing, FastPass+ | ★★★

Astro Orbiter | Before 11 a.m., in the hour before closing | ★★

The Barnstormer *(FastPass+)* | Before 11 a.m., during parades, in the 2 hours before closing, FastPass+ | ★★

Big Thunder Mountain Railroad *(FastPass+)* | Before 10 a.m., in the hour before closing, FastPass+ | ★★★★
　　Special comments 40" minimum height; expectant mothers should not ride

Buzz Lightyear's Space Ranger Spin *(FastPass+)* | First or last hour the park is open, FastPass+ | ★★★★

Captain Jack Sparrow's Pirate Tutorial | Check *Times Guide* for showtimes | ★★★½

Casey Jr. Splash 'N' Soak Station | When it's hot | ★★★

Country Bear Jamboree | Anytime | ★★★½

Dumbo the Flying Elephant *(FastPass+)* | Before 10 a.m., after 6 p.m., FastPass+ | ★★★½

Enchanted Tales with Belle *(FastPass+)* | At opening, in the 2 hours before closing, FastPass+ | ★★★★

Frontierland Shootin' Arcade | Anytime | ★½

The Hall of Presidents (closed until late 2017) | Anytime | ★★★½

The Haunted Mansion *(FastPass+)* | Before 11 a.m., in the 2 hours before closing, FastPass+ | ★★★★½
　　Special comment Fright potential

It's a Small World *(FastPass+)* | Before 11 a.m., during parades, after 7 p.m., FastPass+ | ★★★½

Jungle Cruise *(FastPass+)* | Before 10:30 a.m., in the 2 hours before closing, FastPass+ | ★★★½

Liberty Belle **Riverboat** | Anytime | ★★½

Mad Tea Party *(FastPass+)* | Before 11 a.m., after 5 p.m., FastPass+ | ★★
　　Special comments Expectant mothers should not ride; motion-sickness potential

The Magic Carpets of Aladdin *(FastPass+)* | Before 11 a.m., after 7 p.m., FastPass+ | ★★½

The Many Adventures of Winnie the Pooh *(FastPass+)* | Before 10 a.m., in the hour before closing, FastPass+
　　★★★½

Meet Merida at Fairytale Garden | Check *Times Guide* for schedule | ★★★½

Mickey's PhilharMagic *(FastPass+)* | Before 11 a.m., during parades, FastPass+ | ★★★★

Monsters, Inc. Laugh Floor *(FastPass+)* | Before 11 a.m., after 4 p.m., FastPass+ | ★★★½

Peter Pan's Flight *(FastPass+)* | First or last 30 minutes the park is open, FastPass+ | ★★★★

Pete's Silly Sideshow *(FastPass+)* | Before 11 a.m., in the 2 hours before closing, FastPass+ | ★★★½

A Pirate's Adventure: Treasure of the Seven Seas | Anytime | ★★★½

Pirates of the Caribbean *(FastPass+)* | Before 11 a.m., after 7 p.m., FastPass+ | ★★★★

Prince Charming Regal Carrousel | Anytime | ★★★

Princess Fairytale Hall *(FastPass+)* | Before 10:30 a.m., after 4 p.m., FastPass+ | ★★★

Seven Dwarfs Mine Train *(FastPass+)* | At park opening, FastPass+ | ★★★★

Sorcerers of the Magic Kingdom | Before 11 a.m., after 8 p.m. | ★★★

Space Mountain *(FastPass+)* | At opening, FastPass+ | ★★★★ | *Special comments* 44" minimum height;
expectant mothers should not ride

Splash Mountain *(FastPass+)* | At opening, during parades, just before closing, FastPass+ | ★★★★★
　　Special comments 40" minimum height; expectant mothers should not ride

Stitch's Great Escape! (open seasonally) | Before 11 a.m., during parades, after 6 p.m. | ★★
　　Special comments Fright potential; 40" minimum height

Swiss Family Treehouse | Anytime | ★★★ | *Special comment* Fright potential due to height

Tom Sawyer Island and Fort Langhorn | Midmorning–late afternoon | ★★★

Tomorrowland Speedway *(FastPass+)* | Before 10 a.m., in the 2 hours before closing, FastPass+ | ★★★½
　　Special comment 54" minimum height requirement for kids to drive unassisted

Tomorrowland Transit Authority PeopleMover | Anytime, but especially during hot, crowded times of day
(11:30 a.m.–4:30 p.m.) | ★★★½

Town Square Theater Meet and Greets *(FastPass+)* | Before 10 a.m., after 4 p.m., FastPass+ | ★★★★

Under the Sea: Journey of the Little Mermaid *(FastPass+)* | Before 10:30 a.m., in the 2 hours before closing,
FastPass+ | ★★★½

Walt Disney's Carousel of Progress | Anytime | ★★★

Walt Disney's Enchanted Tiki Room | Before 11 a.m., after 3:30 p.m. | ★★★½

Walt Disney World Railroad | Anytime | ★★★

DINING INFORMATION—Counter Service
RESTAURANT | LOCATION | QUALITY | VALUE | SELECTIONS

Aloha Isle | Adventureland | Excellent | B+ | Dole Whip soft-serve, ice cream floats, pineapple spears, juice

Be Our Guest Restaurant | Fantasyland | Excellent | B+ | *Breakfast:* cured meats and cheeses, bacon-and-egg sandwich, fried doughnuts. *Lunch:* tuna niçoise salad, sandwiches, braised pork with mashed potatoes, veggie quiche, quinoa salad, soup

Casey's Corner | Main Street, U.S.A. | Good | B | Hot dogs, corn dog nuggets, fries, brownies

Columbia Harbour House | Liberty Square | Good | B | Grilled salmon with couscous, fried fish and shrimp, chicken nuggets, sandwiches, clam chowder, vegetarian chili, salads, kids' meals

Cosmic Ray's Starlight Cafe | Tomorrowland | Good | B | Burgers (veggie available), rotisserie chicken and ribs, hot dogs, Greek salad, chicken nuggets, barbecue-pork sandwich; some kosher

The Friar's Nook | Fantasyland | Good | B | Hot dogs, specialty mac and cheese (barbecue chicken, beef pot roast), homemade potato chips, chicken Caesar salad, veggies and chips with hummus, frozen drinks

Gaston's Tavern | Fantasyland | Good | C | Ham and cheese–stuffed pretzels, sliced fruit, mixed veggies with dip, hummus, croissants, cinnamon rolls, LeFou's Brew (frozen apple-juice drink with toasted-marshmallow flavoring)

Golden Oak Outpost *(open seasonally)* | Frontierland | Good | B+ | Waffle fries with various toppings (barbecue pork, slaw, gravy, or cheese), BLT waffle fries, chicken nuggets, cookies

The Lunching Pad | Tomorrowland | Good | B– | Hot dogs, savory pretzels, dessert pretzels, frozen sodas

Pecos Bill Tall Tale Inn & Cafe | Frontierland | Good | C | Steak or chicken fajitas, burritos, rice bowls, salads, soups

The Pinocchio Village Haus | Fantasyland | Fair | C | Pizzas, Italian flatbread sub, chicken nuggets, salads, kids' meals

Tomorrowland Terrace Restaurant *(open seasonally)* | Tomorrowland | Fair | C | Burgers, lobster roll, chicken nuggets, chicken sandwich, salads, kids' meals, cake

Tortuga Tavern *(open seasonally)* | Adventureland | Fair | B | Beef brisket, pork, or grilled chicken sandwiches; roasted corn and vegetable salads; kids' meals; cake, gelato

DINING INFORMATION—Full Service
RESTAURANT | MEALS SERVED | LOCATION | PRICE | QUALITY | VALUE

Be Our Guest Restaurant | B-L-D | Fantasyland | Expensive | ★★★★ | ★★★★
 Selections Catch of the day, grilled strip steak with *pommes frites,* cupcakes, no-sugar-added lemon-raspberry fruit puff

Cinderella's Royal Table | B-L-D | Fantasyland | Expensive | ★★★ | ★★
 Selections Kid's menu; *Breakfast:* French toast, quiche, lobster and shrimp topped with egg and hollandaise, beef cheese frittata; *Lunch:* fish, braised short ribs, pan-seared chicken with polenta; *Dinner:* pork loin, flourless chocolate cake

The Crystal Palace | B-L-D | Main Street, U.S.A. | Moderate | ★★★½ | ★★★
 Selections Buffet (items change often); options may include waffles and pancakes for breakfast; charbroiled octopus, trout, shrimp and grits, salmon, or seafood scampi for lunch or dinner; sundae bar. *Best dining value in the Magic Kingdom*

Jungle Navigation Co. Ltd. Skipper Canteen | L-D | Frontierland | Moderate | ★★★ | ★★★
 Selections Appetizers of hot-and-sour soup, pork and shrimp *shu mai,* falafel balls; entrées of *char siu* pork, lamb chops, shrimp, chicken; kids' meals; chocolate cake, millet-congee pudding, vanilla cake soaked in lemongrass-ginger syrup

Liberty Tree Tavern | L-D | Liberty Square | Moderate | ★★★ | ★★★
 Selections **Lunch:** Pot roast, roast turkey, BLT with pork belly; *Dinner:* all-you-can-eat family-style dining with ham, turkey breast, pot roast, mashed potatoes, stuffing, mac and cheese

The Plaza Restaurant | L-D | Main Street, U.S.A. | Moderate | ★★ | ★★
 Selections Old-fashioned diner and ice cream shop: sandwiches, burgers, salads, sundaes, kids' menu

Tony's Town Square Restaurant | L-D | Main Street, U.S.A. | Moderate | ★★★ | ★★
 Selections Sausage-and-pepperoni flatbread, pasta (gluten-free and whole-grain options), New York strip

Advance Reservations recommended for Magic Kingdom full-service restaurants; call
 ☎ *407-WDW-DINE (939-3463) or visit disneyworld.disney.go.com/reservations/dining.*

GOOD REST AREAS IN THE MAGIC KINGDOM
Back of Storybook Circus, between Big Top Treats and the train station | Fantasyland
 Covered plush seating with electrical outlets and USB charging stations

Covered porch with rocking chairs on Tom Sawyer Island | Frontierland
 Across the water from the *Liberty Belle* Riverboat dock; bring refreshments from Frontierland; closes at sunset

Cul-de-sac | Main Street, U.S.A. | Between the china shop and Main Street's Starbucks on right side of street as you face the castle; nearby refreshments

Picnic tables | Fantasyland | Near the *Tangled*-themed restrooms, between Peter Pan's Flight and The Haunted Mansion; outdoors but has phone-charging stations

Quiet seating area | Tomorrowland | Near restrooms on the right as you approach Space Mountain—look for pay phones, and there's a covered seating area farther back of that corridor; refreshments nearby

Second floor of train station | Main Street, U.S.A. | Refreshments nearby; crowded during fireworks and parades

Upstairs at Columbia Harbour House | Liberty Square | Grab a beverage and relax upstairs; restrooms available

EPCOT **TOURING PLAN COMPANION**

ATTRACTION | LOCATION | RECOMMENDED VISITATION TIMES | AUTHORS' RATING

Agent P's World Showcase Adventure | World Showcase, various pavilions | Anytime | ★★★★

The American Adventure | United States, World Showcase | Anytime | ★★★★

The Circle of Life | The Land, Future World | Anytime | ★★★½

Disney & Pixar Short Film Festival *(FastPass+)* | Imagination! Pavilion, Future World | When raining | —

Epcot Character Spot *(FastPass+)* | Innoventions West, Future World | Before 11 a.m., FastPass+ | ★★★

Frozen Ever After *(FastPass+)* | Norway, World Showcase | Before noon, after 7 p.m., FastPass+ | ★★★★

Gran Fiesta Tour | Mexico, World Showcase | Before noon, after 5 p.m. | ★★½

Impressions de France | France, World Showcase | Anytime | ★★★½

Innoventions East and West | Future World | Second day or after major attractions | ★

Journey Into Imagination with Figment *(FastPass+)* | Imagination! Pavilion, Future World | Anytime | ★★½

Living with the Land *(FastPass+)* | The Land, Future World | Before 11 a.m., after 1 p.m., FastPass+ | ★★★★

Mission: Space *(FastPass+)* | Future World | First or last hour the park is open, FastPass+ | ★★★★
    Special comments 44" minimum height; expectant mothers should not ride; motion-sickness potential

The "Mom, I Can't Believe It's Disney!" Fountains | Future World | When it's hot | ★★★★

O Canada! | Canada, World Showcase | Anytime | ★★★½

Reflections of China | China, World Showcase | Anytime | ★★★½

Royal Sommerhus Meet and Greet | Norway, World Showcase | As soon as it opens, at lunch or dinner, or last hour the park is open | ★★★★

SeaBase | The Seas with Nemo & Friends, Future World | Before 11:30 a.m., after 5 p.m. | ★★★½

The Seas with Nemo & Friends *(FastPass+)* | The Seas with Nemo & Friends, Future World | Before 10:30 a.m., after 3 p.m., FastPass+ | ★★★

Soarin' *(FastPass+)* | The Land, Future World | First 30 minutes the park is open | ★★★★½
    Special comments 40" minimum height; motion-sickness potential

Spaceship Earth *(FastPass+)* | Future World | Before 10 a.m., after 4 p.m., FastPass+ | ★★★★

Test Track *(FastPass+)* | Test Track, Future World | First 30 minutes the park is open, just before closing, FastPass+ | ★★★★ | *Special comments* 40" minimum height; expectant mothers should not ride

Turtle Talk with Crush *(FastPass+)*| The Seas with Nemo & Friends, Future World | Before 11 a.m., after 3 p.m., FastPass+ | ★★★★

Universe of Energy: *Ellen's Energy Adventure* | Future World | Anytime | ★★★½

DINING INFORMATION—Counter Service

RESTAURANT | LOCATION | QUALITY | VALUE | SELECTIONS

L'Artisan des Glaces | France, World Showcase | Excellent | C | Ice cream, sorbet, ice cream sandwiches

La Cantina de San Angel | Mexico, World Showcase | Good | B | Tacos, Mexican salad, grilled chicken with rice and corn, fried cheese empanadas, margaritas, kids' meals, churros, fruit pops

Crêpes des Chefs de France | France, World Showcase | Excellent | B+ | Dessert crepes, ice cream, beer, espresso

Electric Umbrella | Innoventions East, Future World | Fair | B– | Burgers, chicken nuggets, sausage and pepper subs, veggie flatbread, salad with chicken, chicken nuggets, kids' meals, cheesecake, brownies, chocolate cupcake

Fife & Drum Tavern | United States, World Showcase | Fair | C | Turkey legs, popcorn, soft-serve ice cream, frozen slushes, beer

Fountain View | Future World Plaza | Fair | C | Disney-themed Starbucks with all the usual suspects: coffee drinks, teas, breakfast sandwiches, pastries

Les Halles Boulangerie–Pâtisserie | France, World Showcase | Good | A | Pastries, Niçoise salad, cheese plates, sandwiches, quiches, soups

Katsura Grill | Japan, World Showcase | Good | B | Basic sushi; udon noodle bowls; beef, chicken, or salmon teriyaki; chicken curry; miso soup; ice cream (green tea, adzuki bean); green-tea cheesecake; beer, sake, plum wine; teriyaki chicken kids' plate

Kringla Bakeri og Kafe | Norway, World Showcase | Good–excellent | B | Pastries, sandwiches, vegetable torte, rice cream, imported beer and wine

Liberty Inn | United States, World Showcase | Fair | C | Burgers, sandwiches, fried shrimp with rice, salads, hot dogs, chicken nuggets, kids' meals; some kosher

Lotus Blossom Cafe | China, World Showcase | Fair | C | Egg rolls, pot stickers, fried rice, orange chicken, vegetable curry,noodle bowls, caramel-ginger or lychee ice cream, plum wine, Chinese beer

Promenade Refreshments | World Showcase Promenade | Fair | C | Hot dogs, chili dogs, kettle chips, beer

Refreshment Cool Post | Between Germany and China, World Showcase | Good | B– | Hot dogs, soft-serve ice cream, the Doofenslurper (frozen lemonade topped with passion fruit sorbet foam), coffee and tea, beer

Refreshment Port | Near Canada, World Showcase | Good | B- | Croissant doughnuts, chicken nuggets, fries, flavored coffees, hot chocolate, soft-serve ice cream

Rose & Crown Pub | United Kingdom, World Showcase | Good | C+ | Fish-and-chips, chicken masala, bangers and chips, beer

DINING INFORMATION—Counter Service *(continued)*
RESTAURANT | LOCATION | QUALITY | VALUE | SELECTIONS

Sommerfest | Germany, World Showcase | Fair | C | Bratwurst, frankfurter with sauerkraut, baked mac and cheese, cold potato salad, Black Forest cake, beer, wine, schnapps

Sunshine Seasons | The Land, Future World | Excellent | A | Rotisserie and wood-fired meats and fish; salads, sandwiches, soups; Asian noodle bowls and stir-fries; quick breakfast

Tangierine Cafe | Morocco, World Showcase | Good | B | Chicken and lamb shawarma, lentil and couscous salads, hummus, tabbouleh, wraps, kids' meals, wine and beer, baklava

Yorkshire County Fish Shop | United Kingdom, World Showcase | Good | B+ | Fish-and-chips, sponge cake, draft ale

DINING INFORMATION—Full Service
RESTAURANT | MEALS SERVED | LOCATION | PRICE | QUALITY | VALUE

Akershus Royal Banquet Hall | B-L-D | Norway, World Showcase | Expensive | ★★ | ★★★★
  Selections Smoked salmon, herring, mackerel, goat cheese (breakfast); *koldtbord* (buffet of meats, cheeses, seafood, salads), roast chicken, goat-cheese ravioli, pan-seared salmon, *kjottkake* (Norwegian meatballs), kids' menu; full bar

Biergarten | L-D | Germany, World Showcase | Expensive | ★★ | ★★★★
  Selections Buffet with schnitzel, sausages, spaetzle, roast chicken, baked mac and cheese custard, sauerbraten, full bar

Le Cellier Steakhouse | L-D | Canada, World Showcase | Expensive | ★★★½ | ★★★
  Selections Canadian Cheddar cheese soup, steaks, seafood, salmon, full bar

Les Chefs de France | L-D | France, World Showcase | Expensive | ★★★ | ★★★
  Selections Duck breast with cherries, beef tenderloin, Cabernet-braised short ribs, French onion soup, beer and wine

Coral Reef Restaurant | L-D | The Seas with Nemo & Friends, Future World | Expensive | ★★ | ★★
  Selections Creamy lobster soup, steak and seafood, kids' menu, full bar

Garden Grill Restaurant | B-L-D | The Land, Future World | Expensive | ★★★ | ★★★
  Selections Beef filet, turkey with stuffing and gravy, sustainable fish of the day, salads, kids' menu, partial bar service

La Hacienda de San Angel | D | Mexico, World Showcase | Expensive | ★★★½ | ★★½
  Selections *Queso fundido;* pork confit *carnitas;* corn cakes stuffed with chorizo; taco trio; fried-shrimp tacos; full bar

Monsieur Paul | D | France, World Showcase | Expensive | ★★★★½ | ★★★
  Selections Black-truffle soup, red snapper in potato "scales," classic *cassolette d'escargots*, roasted duck breast, full bar

Nine Dragons Restaurant | L-D | China, World Showcase | Moderate | ★★ | ★★
  Selections Braised pork belly steamed buns, Shrimp Typhoon, kung pao shrimp, roast duck salad, five-spice fish, noodles, veggie stir-fry, sticky rice pudding and ginger cake, full bar

Restaurant Marrakesh | L-D | Morocco, World Showcase | Moderate | ★★½ | ★★
  Selections *Bastilla* (minced-chicken pie), shish kebabs, roast lamb, lemon chicken, sampler platters, kids' meals, full bar

Rose & Crown Dining Room | L-D | United Kingdom, World Showcase | Moderate | ★★★½ | ★★
  Selections Fish-and-chips, bangers and mash, shepherd's pie, New York strip steak, sticky toffee pudding, full bar

San Angel Inn Restaurante | L-D | Mexico, World Showcase | Expensive | ★★★ | ★★
  Selections Mole poblano (chicken in chile-chocolate sauce), tacos, tostadas, quesadillas, carne asada, cheesecake, full bar

Spice Road Table | L-D | Morocco, World Showcase | Moderate | ★★★★ | ★★★
  Selections Mediterranean-style small plates; beef and mixed-grill skewers; rack of lamb; yellowfin tuna; ice cream; full bar

Teppan Edo | L-D | Japan, World Showcase | Expensive | ★★★★ | ★★★ |
  Selections Chicken, shrimp, beef, scallops, and veggies stir-fried on teppanyaki grill; full bar

Tokyo Dining | L-D | Japan, World Showcase | Moderate | ★★★★ | ★★★
  Selections Grilled meats and seafood, tempura, sushi, sashimi; full bar

Tutto Gusto Wine Cellar | L-D | Italy, World Showcase | Inexpensive | ★★★ | ★★★
  Selections Cheese plates, charcuterie; pasta, panini; tiramisu, strawberries with mascarpone; wine flights

Tutto Italia Ristorante | L-D | Italy, World Showcase | Expensive | ★★★★ | ★★★
  Selections Pasta, steak, chicken, fried calamari; *panna cotta* and gelato for dessert; beer and wine

Via Napoli | L-D | Italy, World Showcase | Moderate | ★★★½ | ★★★
  Selections Wood-fired pizzas, pastas, salads, sandwiches; beer and wine

Advance Reservations recommended for Epcot full-service restaurants; call ☎ 407-WDW-DINE
(939-3463) or visit disneyworld.disney.go.com/reservations/dining.

GOOD REST AREAS IN EPCOT

Benches | Innovations East and West, Future World | Air-conditioned; usually not crowded

Benches | Mexico, World Showcase | Inside the pavilion against the inside of the wall that forms the walking ramps to the retail space; air-conditioned

Benches | The Seas with Nemo & Friends, Future World | Air-conditioned

Japan gardens | Japan, World Showcase | To the left of Katsura Grill, a set of tables overlooking a lovely garden and koi pond; outdoors but shaded, with refreshments nearby

Rotunda and lobby | United States, World Showcase | Ample room; air-conditioned; refreshments nearby; usually quiet

UK Rose Garden benches | United Kingdom, World Showcase | Behind the UK Pavilion is a small town square and manicured gardens; several outdoor benches available

DISNEY'S ANIMAL KINGDOM **TOURING PLAN COMPANION**

ATTRACTION | RECOMMENDED VISITATION TIMES | AUTHORS' RATING

Avatar Flight of Passage *(FastPass+)* | Before 9:30 a.m., during last 2 hours before closing, FastPass+ | ★★★★½

The Boneyard | Anytime | ★★★

Conservation Station and Affection Section | Anytime | ★★★½

Dinosaur *(FastPass+)* | Before 10:30 a.m., after 4:30 p.m., FastPass+ | ★★★★
Special comments Fright potential; 40" minimum height; expectant mothers should not ride

Expedition Everest *(FastPass+)* | Before 9:30 a.m., after 3 p.m., FastPass+ | ★★★★½
Special comments 44" minimum height; expectant mothers should not ride

Festival of the Lion King (FastPass+) | Before 11 a.m., after 4 p.m., FastPass+ | ★★★★

Flights of Wonder | Anytime | ★★★★

Gorilla Falls Exploration Trail | Anytime | ★★★★

Kali River Rapids *(FastPass+)* | First or last hour the park is open, FastPass+ | ★★★½
Special comments You'll get wet; 38" minimum height; expectant mothers should note that ride is bouncy

Kilimanjaro Safaris *(FastPass+)* | At opening, in the 2 hours before closing | ★★★★★

Maharajah Jungle Trek | Anytime | ★★★★

Meet Favorite Disney Pals at Adventurers Outpost *(FastPass+)* | First thing in the morning, after 5 p.m., FastPass+ | ★★★½

Na'Vi River Journey *(FastPass+)* | Before 9:30 a.m., during the last 2 hours before closing, FastPass+ | ★★★½

The Oasis | Anytime | N/A

Primeval Whirl *(FastPass+)* | First or last hour the park is open, FastPass+ | ★★★
Special comments 48" minimum height; expectant mothers should not ride

Rivers of Light (opens 2016) | Check *Times Guide* for showtimes | ★★★½

Theater in the Wild/*Finding Nemo—The Musical* | Anytime | ★★★★

The Tree of Life/*It's Tough to Be a Bug!/The Awakening* *(FastPass+)* | Anytime, FastPass+ | ★★★★
Special comment Fright potential

TriceraTop Spin | Before noon, after 3 p.m. | ★★

Wilderness Explorers | Sign up first thing in the morning and complete activities throughout the day. | ★★★★

Wildlife Express Train | Anytime | ★★

DINING INFORMATION—**Counter Service**

RESTAURANT | LOCATION | QUALITY | VALUE | SELECTIONS

Creature Comforts | Discovery Island near Africa | Fair | C | Disney-themed Starbucks with all the usual suspects: coffee drinks, teas, breakfast sandwiches, and pastries

Flame Tree Barbecue | Discovery Island | Excellent | B− | Pulled-pork sandwich; ribs; smoked half-chicken; Jamaican jerk chicken salad; watermelon salad; smoked turkey sandwich; fruit plate; child's plate of baked chicken drumstick, hot dog, chicken sandwich, or PB&J sandwich; beer and wine; Key lime or chocolate mousse

Harambe Market | Africa | Good | B | Chicken and beef kebabs with veggie salad; beef and pork or tikka masala chicken sausages with veggie salad; spice-rubbed ribs with veggie salad; South African beer and wine; kids' meals

Kusafiri Coffee Shop and Bakery | Africa | Good | B | Pastries, bagels, hot breakfast wrap, fruit, yogurt, coffee, cocoa, juice; kosher items available

Pizzafari | Discovery Island | Fair | B | Cheese, pepperoni, and veggie pizzas; shrimp flatbread; meatball sub; pasta; salads; kids' meals; chocolate mousse or tiramisu; beer and wine

Restaurantosaurus | DinoLand U.S.A. | Good | B+ | Burgers (good burger-topping bar), hot dog, chicken nuggets, chicken salad, chicken sandwich, kids' meals

Royal Anandapur Tea Company | Asia | Good | B | Hot and iced teas, coffees, lattes, frozen chai, pastries

Satu'li Canteen | Pandora | Too new to rate | Too new to rate | Customizable "bowls" with chicken, beef, fish, or tofu

Thirsty River Bar and Trek Snacks | Asia | Good | B | Smoked turkey or roast pork sandwiches, Thai salad, Asian noodle salad, hummus, fresh fruit and vegetables, ice cream novelties, full bar

Yak & Yeti Local Food Cafes | Asia | Fair | B | Crispy honey chicken with steamed rice, Korean stir-fry barbecue chicken, ginger chicken salad, roasted-vegetable couscous wrap, Asian chicken sandwich; kids' meals of chicken tenders, PB&J, or cheeseburger with fresh fruit

DINING INFORMATION—Full Service
RESTAURANT | MEALS SERVED | LOCATION | PRICE | QUALITY | VALUE

Rainforest Cafe | B-L-D | Park entrance | Moderate | ★★ | ★★
Selections Coconut shrimp, burgers, ribs, brownie cake; breakfast served at this location; full bar

Tiffins | L-D | Discovery Island | Expensive | ★★★★ | ★★★
Selections Appetizers of grilled octopus and black-eyed pea fritters; entrées include whole fried sustainable fish, spiced lamb chops, Wagyu strip loin, duck; lime cheesecake or passion fruit tapioca; full bar

Tusker House Restaurant | B-L-D | Africa | Moderate | ★★★ | ★★★
Selections Rotisserie pork and chicken, carved sirloin, chicken curry, spiced tofu, seafood stew, couscous; character meals; full bar next door

Yak & Yeti Restaurant | L-D | Asia | Expensive | ★★½ | ★★
Selections Lo mein and curry noodle bowls, crispy honey tempura chicken, flat-iron steak, coconut shrimp, chicken tikka masala, teriyaki mahimahi; full bar

Advance Reservations recommended for Animal Kingdom full-service restaurants; call
☎ *407-WDW-DINE (939-3463) or visit disneyworld.disney.go.com/reservations/dining.*

GOOD REST AREAS IN DISNEY'S ANIMAL KINGDOM

Gazebo behind Flame Tree Barbecue | Discovery Island | Follow the path toward the water, along the left side of Flame Tree Barbecue; gazebo has ceiling fans

Outdoor covered benches near exit from Dinosaur | DinoLand U.S.A. | Gazebo-like structure with nearby water fountain

Seating area adjacent to Dawa Bar | Africa | Refreshments nearby; outdoors and can be noisy from street performers

Walkway between Africa and Asia | Between Africa and Asia | Plenty of shaded rest spots, some overlooking streams; refreshments nearby; a favorite of *Unofficial Guide* researchers

DISNEY'S HOLLYWOOD STUDIOS **TOURING PLAN COMPANION**

ATTRACTION | RECOMMENDED VISITATION TIMES | AUTHORS' RATING

Alien Swirling Saucers *(not open at press time)* | As soon as the park opens

Disney Junior—Live on Stage! (FastPass+) | Per entertainment schedule | ★★★★

Fantasmic! (FastPass+) | Check *Times Guide* for schedule; if 2 shows are offered, 2nd show is less crowded. | ★★★★½

For the First Time in Forever: A Frozen Sing-Along Celebration (FastPass+) | Arrive 15 minutes before showtime | ★★★

The Great Movie Ride (FastPass+) | Before 11 a.m., during dinner, after 8 p.m., FastPass+ | ★★★½

Indiana Jones Epic Stunt Spectacular! (FastPass+) | First 2 shows or last show | ★★★½

Jedi Training: Trials of the Temple | First 2 shows | ★★★½

Jim Henson's Muppet-Vision 3-D (FastPass+) | Anytime | ★★★★

Rock 'n' Roller Coaster (FastPass+) | First 30 minutes the park is open, FastPass+ | ★★★★
   Special comments 48" minimum height; expectant mothers should not ride; kids under age 7 must ride with an adult

Slinky Dog Coaster (FastPass+; not open at press time) | As soon as the park opens, FastPass+

Star Tours—The Adventures Continue (FastPass+) | Before 10 a.m., after 6 p.m., FastPass+ | ★★★½
   Special comments Fright potential; 40" minimum height; expectant mothers should not ride; motion-sickness potential

Star Wars Launch Bay (FastPass+) | Anytime, FastPass+ | ★★

Theater of the Stars/Beauty and the Beast—Live on Stage (FastPass+) | Anytime | ★★★★

Toy Story Mania! (FastPass+) | At opening, FastPass+ | ★★★★½

The Twilight Zone Tower of Terror (FastPass+) | First or last 30 minutes the park is open,
   FastPass+ | ★★★★★ | *Special comments* 40" minimum height; expectant mothers should not ride

Voyage of the Little Mermaid (FastPass+) | Before 9:45 a.m., just before closing, FastPass+ | ★★★½

Walt Disney: One Man's Dream | Anytime | ★★★

DINING INFORMATION—**Counter Service**
RESTAURANT | LOCATION | QUALITY | VALUE | SELECTIONS

ABC Commissary | Commissary Lane | Fair | B– | New York strip steak, Asian salad (chicken optional), Angus cheeseburger, chicken club sandwich, shrimp or seafood platter, kids' meals, some kosher, chocolate mousse, cupcakes, beer and wine

Backlot Express | Echo Lake | Fair | C | Angus cheeseburger (with or without brisket on top); chicken nuggets; chicken and waffles; chicken salad; garlic Parmesan fries, chili-cheese dog, Star Wars–themed desserts

Catalina Eddie's | Sunset Boulevard | Fair | B | Cheese and pepperoni pizzas; chicken pesto flatbread; Caesar salad; banana parfait; vanilla cake with chocolate custard

Fairfax Fare | Sunset Boulevard | Fair | B | Barbecue chicken, ribs, and pulled-pork sandwiches; "designer" hot dogs; chili dogs; loaded baked potatoes; Fairfax salad with barbecue pork, bacon, and corn-tomato salsa; banana parfait; vanilla cake

Min and Bill's Dockside Diner | Echo Lake | Fair | C | Slow-roasted beef with mashed potatoes, corn, and carrots; chili-cheese dog with chips; mac and cheese with pulled pork; sushi veggie roll with edamame salad; chocolate cake; kids' meal of turkey sandwich, carrots, and cookie

PizzeRizzo | Muppet Courtyard | Poor | D | Pizza, salads, cookies, cupcakes

Rosie's All-American Cafe | Sunset Boulevard | Fair | C | Burgers; fried green tomato sandwich on ciabatta bread; chicken nuggets; soups; child's turkey sandwich or chicken nuggets with carrot sticks or applesauce; strawberry shortcake or vanilla cake with chocolate custard

Trolley Car Cafe | Sunset Boulevard | Fair | C | Disney-themed Starbucks with all the usual suspects: coffee drinks, teas, breakfast sandwiches, and pastries

DINING INFORMATION—**Full Service**
RESTAURANT | MEALS SERVED | LOCATION | PRICE | QUALITY | VALUE

50's Prime Time Cafe | L-D | Echo Lake | Moderate | ★★★ | ★★★
   Selections Pot roast, chicken potpie, meat loaf, fried chicken; PB&J milk shake; full bar

Hollywood & Vine | B-L-D | Echo Lake | Moderate | ★★★ | ★★★
   Selections Salads, soups, fish of the day, carved and grilled meats, vegetables and pasta, fresh fruits and breads, sundae bar and chocolate fountain (menu changes often); character breakfast and lunch; full bar

The Hollywood Brown Derby | L-D | Hollywood Boulevard | Expensive | ★★★★ | ★★★
   Selections Cobb salad, pan-seared black grouper, char-glazed beef filet, Wagyu-beef burger, fettuccine Alfredo, grapefruit cake, kids' menu. Patio lounge serves cocktails and small plates.

Mama Melrose's Ristorante Italiano | L-D | Muppet Courtyard | Moderate | ★★★ | ★★
   Selections Penne alla vodka, seasonal pastas, charred strip steak, oak-fired mussels, tiramisu and cannolis

Sci-Fi Dine-In Theater Restaurant | L-D | Commissary Lane | Moderate | ★★½ | ★★
   Selections Sandwiches, burgers, salads, shakes; pasta, ribs, steak

*Advance Reservations recommended for DHS full-service restaurants; call ☎ 407-WDW-DINE
   (939-3463) or visit disneyworld.disney.go.com/reservations/dining.*

GOOD REST AREAS IN DISNEY'S HOLLYWOOD STUDIOS

Animation Building | Animation Courtyard | Benches in and around Star Wars Launch Bay; refreshments nearby

Benches along Echo Lake | Echo Lake | Some are shaded; refreshments nearby

Covered seating behind Toluca Legs Turkey Company | Sunset Boulevard | Refreshments nearby; ample seating

Tune-In Lounge | Echo Lake, next to 50's Prime Time Cafe | Air-conditioned bar; nonalcoholic drinks and food from 50's Prime Time Cafe also available (Thanks to Matt Hochberg of studioscentral.com for this tip.)